EUROPEAN FOOTBALL STADIUMS

EUROPEAN FOOTBALL STADIUMS

MICHAEL HEATLEY

First published in 2006 by Compendium Publishing Ltd

ISBN: 1-905573-00-6

Printed and Bound in China by Constant Printing Limited

COVER: The Olympic Stadium in Berlin will host the World Cup final on 9 July 2006.

PAGE 2: Goal! Let's hope there are plenty of them in 2006. This one was scored during the Group B Confederations Cup match between Greece and Mexico at the Waldstadion, Frankfurt, on 22 June 2005.

BELOW: Fans watch the Bundesliga match between Hertha BSC and Werder Bremen at Berlin's Olympic Stadium in November 2004.

Photo Credits
Most photos were provided by Getty Images—thanks to Marc Seigerman for all his help. The remainder are as credited below: *AFP/Getty Images* pp 8, 10, 26, 30, 32, 34, 36, 34, 36, 45, 52, 54, 56, 64, 66, 80, 106, 108, 120, 123, 126, 127, 135, 155, 172, 184, 187, 188, 192, 194, 207, 210, 211, 212, 214, 215, 217, 232, 234, 245, 250, 252. *Bongarts/Getty Images* pp 2, 5–14, 16–25, 27–29, 31, 37–39, 40–42, 44, 46–51, 57–63, 68–79, 90, 92, 94. 119, 124, 132–133, 138, 152, 174, 195, 200, 201, 218, 220, 230. *Man Utd via Getty Images* pp 104, 178, 180, 182, 183. *EMPICS: Matthew Ashton* pp 120, 134, 222. *Fotolibra:* Alison Utsunomiya p 98. *Corbis:* Maury Christian/Corbis Sygma p 102; Vernier Jean Bernard/Corbis Sigma p 206; Amebicque Bernard/Corbis Sigma p 208; Philippe Coron/Corbis Sigma p 209; Stephane Reix/For Picture p 196; Edward Boone/For Picture p 199; Manuel Blondeau/Photo & Co p 103; Vincent van Doormick/Photo & Co pp 91, 94; Reuters pp1, 229; Bogdan Christel/Reuters p 244; Christian Charisius/Reuters p 33; Christian Liewig p 198; Daniele La Monaca/Reuters p 82; Fabrizio Bensch/Reuters p 43; Jose Manuel Ribeiro/Reuters p 236; Stephen Hird/ Reuters p 254; Ralf-Finn Hestoft p 6; Yann Arthus-Bertrand p 204

Thanks to Rasmus Dahlberg and Susanne Willers for researching the photos on pp 110, 111, 154 (Helsinki Stadion Management Oy), 176 (Malmö Stadion), 177 (Malmö Stadion), 232 (FK Shakhtar Donetsk).

Contents

Introduction

In terms of money, prestige and the share of the sporting media it commands, football is probably in better shape in the current millennium than at any time in its recent history. While the game's 'gentrification' has not gone down well in some quarters, including FIFA president Sepp Blatter, increased ticket prices have had the effect of reducing organised violence around the fringes of the game.

Seated stadiums have also quelled inflamed passions, if sometimes at the cost of atmosphere. It's interesting that some counties have allowed the reintroduction of standing terracing, though this is still not permitted in European competition.

One thing is for certain—the 'bar' has been raised in terms of the facilities spectators demand of football stadia, leading for instance to the lengthy redevelopment of England's national stadium at Wembley, while the quest for higher capacity and increased revenue has led clubs like Arsenal to develop new grounds entirely. The biggest single catalyst, however, was the awarding of the 2006 World Cup to Germany, which has led not only to new grounds being built but the refurbishment of existing venues.

If a larger proportion of the money entering the game through deals with television companies could be spent on infrastructure rather than being recycled into the pockets of players and their agents, then the process could be speeded up considerably. Until then, naming rights and other devices will have to suffice.

With the former Eastern bloc now firmly under the European football umbrella, the general level of comfort and amenity at the continent's football ground is rising all the time. This book takes a snapshot of the overall situation at the halfway point in the decade—look out for further changes in the future.

Michael Heatley

Note on the photographs

The Author and Publisher would like to thank Getty Images for their help with the majority of the material for this book. Wherever possible we have used up-to-date images of the stadiums. While most of the stadiums in this book are club grounds, we have also inserted for interest some images of national grounds such as Belgium's on page 95, France's on page 209, Israel's on page 174, Turkey's on page 142 and,of course, Wembley on page 254.

RIGHT: Germany has a proud record in the World Cup and the team is well-supported wherever it plays. Here, German and Bolivian soccer fans wave banners and flags at the opening ceremony of the 1994 World Cup at Chicago's Soldier Field.

GERMANY
BOLIVIA
HALF
:00
0
0
2
S.V.
RM NY
D CHAMPIONS
Grüße an
MANNHEIM
RUSSIA
BORUSSIA

Section 1: German venues for the 2006 World Cup

FC Bayern Munich/TSV 1860 Munich

Stadium:	Allianz Arena
Address:	Werner-Heisenberg-Allee 25, 80939 München
Website:	www.allianz-arena.de
Ground capacity:	66,000
Opening date:	30 May 2005
Architect:	Herzog and de Meuron
Most important games:	Will hold the opening game of the 2006 FIFA World Cup

The newest and most expensive of the 12 World Cup stadia at a cost of 280 million euros, the Allianz Arena in Munich opened its doors for the first time on 30 May 2005 for a game between TSV 1860 Munich and FC Nuremberg, followed the day after by the Arena's other tenants—FC Bayern Munich, taking on the German national team.

The brand new stadium was designed by celebrity Swiss architects Jacques Herzog and Pierre de Meuron, after plans to renovate Munich's old ground, the Olympiastadion, was rejected. Whatever they came up with had a monumental act to follow—the Olympiastadion was once the best stadium in West Germany, then the whole of Germany, with its innovative tent-like roof design.

The new stadium is their idea of a futuristic football stadium, its one of a kind bubble-like design made up of no less than 2,874 inflatable foil cushions that are UV-permeable, and unaffected by any weather conditions. These cushions act as a projection surface to bathe the stadium in either red or blue, depending on which of its tenants are playing at the time—Bayern Munich or TSV 1860 Munich.

While insurance company Allianz holds the naming rights to the stadium until 2021, the tenants have let it be known the term alliance also represents the friendship between the two clubs.

The Olympiastadion hosted the third-place play-off match and the final on consecutive days the last time the World Cup came to Germany. The impressive Allianz Arena will have the honour of staging the 2006 tournament's opening fixture, followed by three more group games, a knockout game and a semi-final.

PREVIOUS PAGE: The Olympic Stadium in Berlin.

RIGHT: Spectacular dusk view of Munich's new Allianz Arena during a lighting test.

Allianz Arena

Above: Home to FC Bayern Munich and TSV 1860 Munich, the Allianz Arena's outer shell has the ability to change colour according to which team is playing.

Left: A view of the roof of the Allianz Arena football stadium. Built at a cost of euro 275 million, it will host the first of the 2006 Football World Cup matches.

Previous page, left: An exhibition match between 1860 Munich and Bayern Munich at the Allianz Arena on 19 May 2005 before the official opening. Former players from both clubs came together for the first match to be played in the stadium.

Previous page, right: The arena was opened in May 2005 and seats 60,000.

Borussia Dortmund

Stadium:	Westfalenstadion
Address:	Strobelallee 50, 44139 Dortmund
Website:	www.borussia-dortmund.de
Ground capacity:	82,000 (69,000 for international games)
Opening date:	1974, modified in 2003
Architect:	Planungsgruppe Drahtler
Nickname:	The Opera House
Most important games:	Hosted 1974 World Cup matches with a team outside the German top division. World Cup 2006 venue
Memorable moments:	First game ended 0–3 against Schalke 04

Officially the largest stadium in Germany, the Westfalenstadion's most interesting feature is undoubtedly its terraced south stand for Borussia Dortmund's passionate supporters. Holding 25,000 spectators, it is a rare sight in top-flight football, and has been described as a 'real feeling of community', as when sold out, three spectators share the space of an unfolded broadsheet newspaper. Not to be left behind, the 'Südtribühne' can be converted into a 10,500-seater stand within two days, for when Dortmund enter into European competition or host a major European final, as they did in 2001, holding the UEFA Cup final at the Westfalenstadion.

Built in 1974 specifically for the World Cup, what has become known as the Opera House underwent redevelopment in 2002–03, where the ground's four stands were joined together to increase the capacity in preparation for the same competition 32 years later. Additionally, the rigid barriers behind the goals were replaced with a new flexible fence system. Bundesliga 1 side and Champions League winners Dortmund hold the record for the most amount of fans during a season at over a million, though they weren't always that successful in the Westfalenstadion.

During the World Cup in 1974, Dortmund were in the second tier of German football after being relegated, yet had a brand new ground and were hosting international football. Host to six matches at the 2006 World Cup, including a semi-final, fans will be hard pushed to miss this grand structure, not least because of its eight bright, Borussia Dortmund-coloured yellow pylons that hold the roof up.

RIGHT: A Bundesliga game in April 2005 between Borussia Dortmund and Bayer Leverkusen.

LG
Flatron LCD
LG
Flatron Plasma
LG
Waschmaschinen
LG
Kühlgeräte
LG
Heimkino
LG
Flatron LCD
GARDINIA
GARDINIA
SIGNAL IDUNA
SIGNAL IDUNA

RIGHT: The Westfalenstadion seats 82,000 for Bundesliga fixtures and 69,000 for international games. The differential is due to standing areas being permitted for domestic games.

BELOW: Dortmund players warm up before a match against VFL Bochum. The home side lost 0-1.

LG
Heimkino
Flatron LCD
Flatron Plasma
Waschmaschinen
BVB

Südtribüne

LEFT: An exterior view of Dortmund's impressive Westfalenstadion.

BELOW: Borussia Dortmund fans show their support during the Bundesliga clash against FC Cologne in September 2005.

Eintracht Frankfurt

Stadium:	Commerzbank Arena
Address:	Moerfelder Landstrasse 362, 60528 Frankfurt
Website:	www.eintracht.de
Ground capacity:	52,000 (8,000 standing)
Opening date:	1920, rebuilt 2005
Architect:	Gerkan, Marg und Partner
Nickname:	The Opera House
Most important games:	Venue for 1974 World Cup and 1988 European Championships; venue for 2006 World Cup
Memorable moments:	First Match—Local XI versus Boca Juniors 24 May 1925

Famous for the Muhammad Ali versus Karl Mildenberger world boxing bout in 1966, and even more so for the waterlogged World Cup semi-final between Poland and West Germany in 1974 where a helicopter was employed to attempt to dry out the playing surface, the Waldstadion in Frankfurt was originally built on an old army shooting range. Its location in the middle of a forest, or wald, gives the stadium its name.

The shooting range was deactivated as ordered in the Treaty of Versailles in 1919, and the stadium built in its place was renovated for the 1974 World Cup and 1988 European Championships. A third renovation was applied for in 2001, but with World Cup 2006 on the horizon the city council decided to go ahead with building a whole new stadium on the site. This was completed in time for the 2005 Confederations Cup and the 2005-06 Bundesliga season.

The Waldstadion is home to Bundesliga side Eintracht Frankfurt and NFL Europe outfit Frankfurt Galaxy, both of which used the stadium during the construction period—rebuilding took place in stages so games could still go ahead with a reduced capacity of 30,000.

Named the Commerzbank Arena after a naming deal with a Frankfurt-based bank, among the 52,000 capacity stadium's new features is a giant video cube, suspended some 25 metres above the pitch; with each screen 30 square metres, the crowd should never miss a kick. Frankfurt's bigwigs will be hoping the stadium can be used for a wide range of sports and entertainment purposes, the Waldstadion's moveable roof allowing some indoor events. Athletics usage will be limited, however, after the removal of the running track around the pitch.

RIGHT: An aerial view of Frankfurt's Commerzbank Arena during the Confederations Cup match between Greece and Japan on 19 June 2005.

FLYING EAGLES
DIGITAL
DIGITAL
Adecco
Adecco

Mainova
Mainova
Adecco
Adecco

FRANKFURT
PHILIPS
HYUNDAI
adidas
FRANKFURT
TOSHIBA
FUJIFILM
PHILIPS
AVAYA
FUJIFILM

LEFT: The Commerzbank Arena is pictured during a training session of the German national team on the eve of the Confederations Cup. They came third in the tournament after beating Mexico 4-3.

ABOVE: Eintracht Frankfurt play SpVgg Greuther Fuerth on 21 March 2005.

PREVIOUS PAGE: A view of the Commerzbank Arena during the Bundesliga match between Eintracht Frankfurt and Bayern Munich in September 2005.

Hamburg

Stadium:	AOL Arena
Formerly:	Volksparkstadion
Address:	Sylvester Allee 7, 22525 Hamburg
Website:	www.hsv.de
Ground capacity:	55,000 (10,000 standing)
Opening date:	1953, reopened September 2000
Architect:	Mos Architekten
Most important games:	World Cup 2006 venue
Memorable moments:	Opened in September 2000 with a showcase match of Germany versus. Greece

One of only three German stadiums to hold the coveted 'five-star' award by UEFA, the Volksparkstadion—or as it's officially known, the AOL Arena—is one of the best grounds in the country, eligible to host the UEFA Cup, or Champions League Final. Its status was further confirmed when chosen to host one of the World Cup quarter finals in 2006.

The stadium is no stranger to international competition, having held group matches in the 1974 World Cup, plus a semi-final in the European Championship in 1988 when hosts West Germany fell to the Netherlands—the only match the stadium held in the whole tournament. Home to Bundesliga side Hamburg SV, the ground was demolished in four stages and re-opened in September 2000 with Germany hosting Greece in an international match. During redevelopment, the pitch was rotated 90 degrees as to make the most of the sunlight and to give the 55,000-capacity stadium's fans a better view of the match.

The track and field facilities around the pitch were also got rid of. There was some distance between the old east and west stands behind the goals and the pitch before the renovation—and the players used to enter from a tunnel in the middle of the West Stand. Terraces still have a part to play in the new arena, with 10,000 standing places. These can be converted into seats for European and international competition by means of a mechanism which rotates the terracing 180 degrees to be replaced by steps with seats on.

Although internet giants AOL bought the naming rights to the Volksparkstadion in 2001, many of Hamburg's passionate supporters prefer to call it by its original name which translates to the People's Park.

RIGHT: Hamburg train at the AOL Arena in December 2004.

www.mopo.de
MOPO. So ist das.
AOLARENA
simply worldwide BIRKART GLOBISTICS
www.birkart.com
HAMBURG 1
RADIO HAMBURG
www.hsv.de
BAUHAUS
BG-Haus.de
SIGNAL IDUN

AOL A

Left: Hamburg's AOL Arena has a seating capacity of 55,000, including 10,000 standing places.

Below: A match in progress at the AOL Arena.

LEFT: A German supporter waves his county's flag during the Germany-China friendly, 12 October 2005.

ABOVE: Hamburg SV's head coach Thomas Doll acknowledges fans after his team beat SC Freiburg 4–0 in the Bundesliga, October 2004.

Hannover 96

Stadium:	AWD Arena
Formerly:	Niedersachsenstadion
Address:	Clausewitzstrasse 2, 30175 Hannover
Website:	www.awd-arena.de
Ground capacity:	49,000 (7,000 standing)/45,000 all-seater for European and Internationals
Opening date:	1954
Architect:	Helmut C. Schulitz (redevelopment)
Nickname:	The Opera House
Most important games:	World Cup 2006 venue
Memorable moments:	First International game: Germany v France, 16 October 1954

Another ground to have featured in the 1974 World Cup, with both Brazil and the Netherlands playing there, the Niedersachsenstadion (Lower Saxony Stadium), was reconstructed for the international visits in 2006. Instantly recognisable thanks to its 'wavy' appearance, and costing some 60 million euros to built, it has been home to Bundesliga 1 side Hannover 96 for over 40 years.

The old stadium was built with two million cubic metres of rubble from World War Two after the city of Hamburg was destroyed. It used to hold some 86,000 people, with the majority under cover, and famous for its thin, leaning floodlights, but the presence of a running track around the pitch limited the atmosphere. It is now a purpose-built, football-only stadium even sporting a roof, having formerly being a multi-purpose arena. It now holds 49,000 spectators for Hannover's league games, and the 7,000 capacity standing terrace is, like many other WC 2006 stadia, converted into seating to bring the total capacity down to 45,000.

The AWD Arena will host three initial group matches and one knock-out game in the 2006 World Cup, so as many as eight of the 32 international teams will visit the new arena. It is situated in an idyllic setting, right next to the Masch Lake, with a view of the Hannover town hall dome visible from the seats of the old ground. Welding firm AWD purchased the rights to name the new stadium, naming it the AWD Arena upon its inauguration in January 2005. However, like all sponsored stadiums hosting World Cup matches, the AWD Arena will operate during the tournament under its original name of World Cup Arena Hannover.

RIGHT: The AWD Arena on 26 June 2005 during the 2005 FIFA Confederations Cup semi-final between Mexico and Argentina.

adidas
Fly Emirates
TOSHIBA
HYUNDAI
T-Mobile
YAHOO!
PHILIPS
ODDSET
NNOVER

AWD arena

LEFT AND ABOVE: Two aerial views of the AWD-Arena taken on 16 September 2005.

PAGE 38: Inside the AWD-Arena as Hannover 96 beat Borussia Moenchengladbach 2–1 on 19 March 2005.

PAGE 39: The Niedersachsenstadion in Hanover as it was before modernisation, the running track clearly visible.

WÜRTH
TUI.de
AWD Ihr unabhängiger Finanzoptimierer AWD

DiaNorm
VGH
Einbecker
CORNY
Gilde

Hertha BSC Berlin

Stadium:	The Olympic Stadium
Address:	Olympischer Platz 3, 14053 Berlin–Charlottenburg
Website:	www.herthabsc.de
Ground capacity:	74,500
Opening date:	1936. Renovated: 31 July 2004
Architect:	Werner March
Most important games:	World Cup Final 2006 venue
Memorable moments:	Built for the 1936 Nazi Olympic games

Originally a horse-racing track, the Olympic Stadium in Berlin was originally converted to host the 1916 Olympic games, cancelled due to the first world war. It finally hosted the Olympics 20 years later. The 1936 games are memorable for black American runner Jesse Owens winning four gold medals, much to the ruling Nazi regime's displeasure, and today one of the avenues leading to the arena displays his name.

This is unlike any other football stadium, catering as it does for Olympic hockey, swimming and track events. Perhaps its most striking feature is the some 25-metre wide Marathon Gate from which the nearby bell tower can be viewed.

The arrival of Hertha BSC Berlin in the early 1960s coincided with the foundation of the Bundesliga, and the stadium has since enjoyed top-flight domestic and European football, Berlin regularly qualifying for the UEFA Cup since the turn of the millennium. The ground's annual showpiece event since 1985 has undoubtedly been the DFB Pokal Final, Germany's domestic Cup Final which attracts nationwide interest.

The Olympic stadium hosted three games in the 1974 World Cup for which it received a 'make-over', including a new floodlight system and a Plexiglas roof. With Berlin getting the nod to host the 2006 World Cup Final, the Olympic Stadium's biggest renovation commenced in 2000 and took four years to fully complete. A deal struck with Walter Bau, the firm behind the huge refurbishment task, ensured a capacity of at least 55,000 would be available at all times, so the daily operations of the stadium were not adversely affected. Indeed, over 100 events were held at the ground during the refurbishment period, including the 2001 Cup Final.

Right: The Olympic Stadium—the venue for glory.

Page 42: Germany 1 Brazil 1 in the Olympic Stadium in September 2004.

Page 43: The renovated Olympic Stadium during the Bundesliga match between Vfl Bochum and Hertha Berlin in August 2004.

OMEGA

Buderus

herthabsc.de
Bewag
Krombacher
1892

ABOVE: Exterior view of Berlin's Olympic Stadium on the evening of its official inauguration, 31 July 2004.

LEFT: A 1996 view of the Olympic Stadium before its multi-million-euro renovation.

FC Kaiserslautern

Stadium:	Fritz-Walter Stadion
Address:	Fritz Walter Strasse 11, 67653 Kaiserslautern
Website:	www.fck.de
Ground capacity:	48,500
Opening date:	1926, renovation 2002–03
Architect:	Fiebiger Engineering
Nickname:	The Betzenberg
Most important games:	World Cup 2006 venue
Memorable moments:	Germany versus. Hungary 2004 —50th anniversary of 1954 World Cup

Named after the national captain in the 1954 World Cup, who played for just one team in a career spanning some 31 years, it was fitting that a redeveloped Fritz-Walter Stadion was on the cards when Germany was awarded the 2006 World Cup.

The ground, home to Bundesliga side FC Kaiserslautern, imposes its presence on the city from its position up in the mountains, underwent a near-50 million euro renovation that included new floodlight and loudspeaker systems, as well as integrating technology for the media in the North Stand—one of the core requirements set by FIFA for a stadium hosting a World Cup match. The ground's east and west corners were also extended.

The Betzenberg gained its nickname after the mountain the ground is built on, and it was also the name of the stadium until it was renamed in honour of the German football hero in 1985. It was once famous for its ferocious fans and intimidating atmosphere, its reputation peaking in the 80s after Bayern Munich lost there 7–4 after leading 1–4 at half-time. Since that game, the Fritz Walter Stadion has not boasted such a frightening atmosphere due to troubles on and off the pitch causing empty seats and therefore less atmosphere. However 1.FK fans can boast that their side have only been out of the top division for one year in their entire history, winning the championship immediately after being re-promoted. Fans will be hoping the club and ground's reputation will be restored to their former glory after the Fritz-Walter showcases its new features in its 2006 World Cup matches.

RIGHT: Fans await the arrival of FC Kaiserslautern and Bayern Munich at the Fritz-Walter Stadium in April 2004.

PAGE 48–49: A 1998 view of the Fritz-Walter Stadium during a fine 2–1 win for the home side over Borussia Moenchengladbach.

sche Vermögensberatung
Deutsche Vermögensberatung
Deutsche Vermögensberatung
Deutsche Vermögensberatung
Deutsche Vermögensberatung

2 : 1
NISSAN

ABOVE: Kaiserslautern fans show their colours before the match against Hamburg in October 2005.

RIGHT: View from the stands of the Betzenberg.

WURTH

FC Köln (Cologne)

Stadium:	Rheinenergie Stadion, Mungersdorfer Stadion
Address:	Aachener Strasse 999, 50933 Köln
Website:	www.stadion-koeln.de
Ground capacity:	50,000 (45,000 for internationals)
Opening date:	16 September 1923, renovated in 1975 and 2004
Architect:	Von Gerkan, Marg and Partner
Most important games:	World Cup 2006 venue
Memorable moments:	Inaugural game—31 March 2004 Germany versus Belgium

Originally intended to create 15,000 jobs after the Treaty of Versailles at the end of the First World War, the Mungersdorfer Stadion quickly gathered respect and prominence in the city. It was hailed as Germany's first completely covered stadium upon its reconstruction in 1975, with a low, cantilever roof covering the elliptical stadium. Unfortunately it was one year too late to host any games in the 1974 World Cup, because the cost of renovation was too high.

The second incarnation of the Mungersdorfer Stadium in Cologne did host international competition in 1988, the highlight being the Netherlands playing eventual finalists the Soviet Union in the European Championships. When it became known that Germany would host the World Cup finals, the stadium underwent a '21st century facelift'—a third reconstruction at a cost of 110 million euros. As with many other stadiums, the financial burden of rebuilding was eased by the sale of naming rights; it was rechristened the Rheinenergie Stadium after a deal was struck with the energy company.

Work began on the ground in late 2001 after Bundesliga side FC Köln had played their last game of the year. But FC Köln and NFL Europe side Köln Centurions were able to play their home matches at the Mungersdorfer throughout the construction period. Like most arenas that used to be multi-purpose sports venues before football took precedence, the running track surrounding the playing field was scrapped, and the ground now follows the British model of allowing the crowds closer to the action. The new stadium has a completely different, rectangular shape to its predecessor, punctuated by four posts in each corner like a boxing ring. The German national side has since played its home matches in the stadium, with quite an impressive record.

RIGHT: General view of the Rheinenergie Stadium in June 2005 prior to the Confederations Cup match between Germany and Tunisia.

adidas

The Rheinenergie Stadium before the Confederations Cup match between Japan and Brazil.

SUBSTITUTES
BRAZIL
McDonald's
HYUNDAI
T · Mobile
YAHOO!
PHILIPS
TOSHIBA
MasterCard
ODDSET
OBI
OBI
EnBW

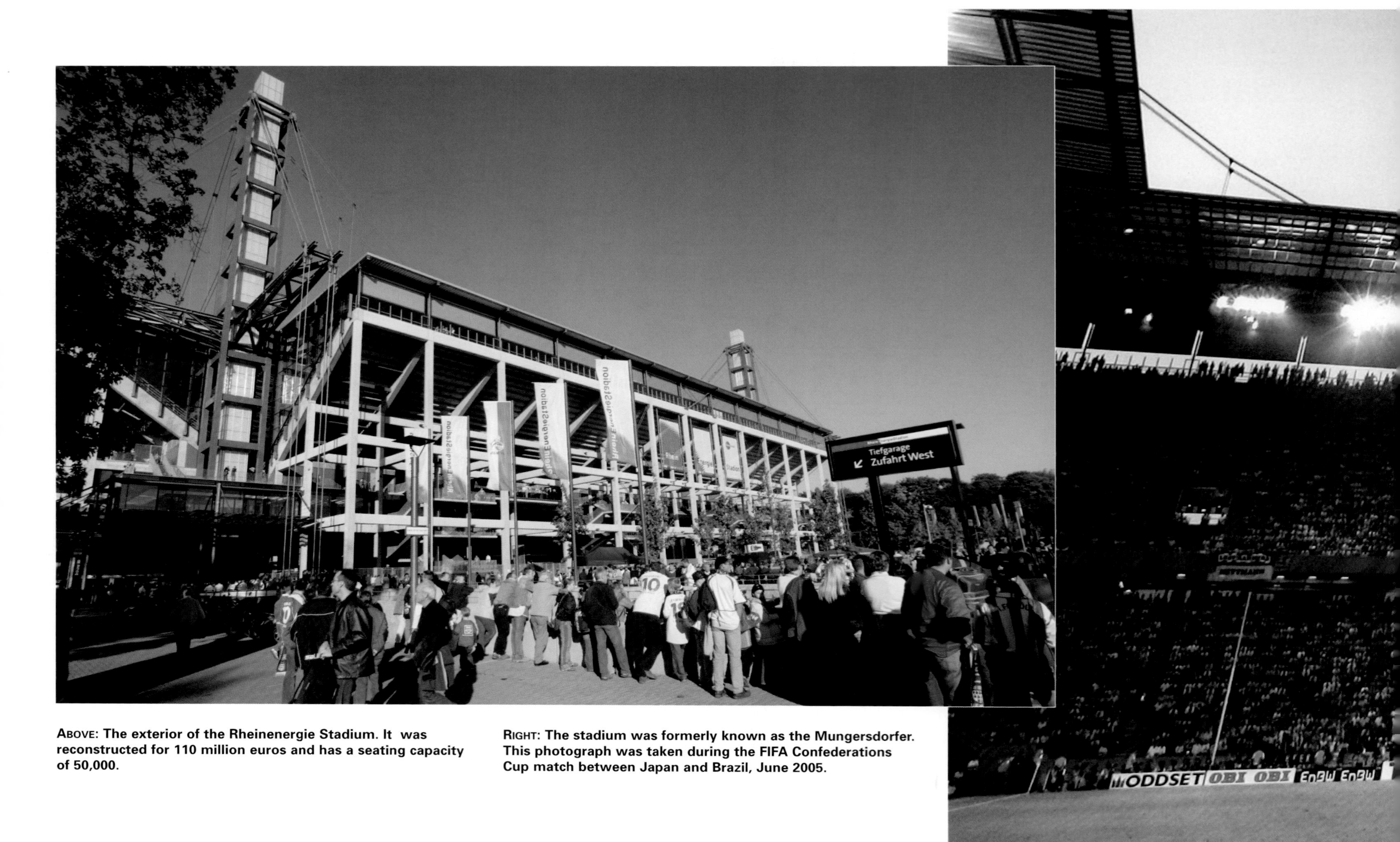

ABOVE: The exterior of the Rheinenergie Stadium. It was reconstructed for 110 million euros and has a seating capacity of 50,000.

RIGHT: The stadium was formerly known as the Mungersdorfer. This photograph was taken during the FIFA Confederations Cup match between Japan and Brazil, June 2005.

Fly Emirates
HYUNDAI
adidas

FC Sachsen Leipzig

Stadium:	Zentralstadion
Address:	Am Sportforum 3, 04105 Leipzig
Website:	www.zentralstadion-le.de
Ground capacity:	44,000
Opening date:	1956, reopened 7 March 2004
Architect:	Wirth + Wirth and consortium
Most important games:	World Cup 2006 venue
Memorable moments:	17 November 2004 Germany versus. Cameroon, 16 years after the last international game was played there.

Without doubt one of the most impressive purpose-built football stadiums out of the chosen 12 for the 2006 World Cup, the Zentralstadion in Leipzig should surely be playing host to football at the highest level week in and week out. In reality, the ground is home to German third division side FC Sachsen Leipzig. The DFB, or German FA, was founded in Leipzig, which might help explain its prominence.

The 44,000-seater stadium, whose name predictably translates as Central Stadium, is holding four group matches and one knockout game this summer, but it could have hosted more prestigious games had its attendance been higher. When the first version of the Zentralstadion was built from the rubble of the Second World War in as little as 15 months it had the largest capacity of any stadium in Germany with 100,000, and known throughout the world as 'the stadium of the one hundred thousand'.

When the country was divided, the Zentralstadion was the venue where East Germany played its first ever competitive match, against Wales in a World Cup qualifier in 1957. But over time the stadium fell into disuse, with weeds growing out of the terraces and sections of the stands ripped away completely. One fan who broke into the stadium said it was like 'an apocalyptic movie where all the humans are gone and nature takes over'. The stadium had obviously become a burden to the town, so in 2000, with the World Cup on the horizon, the decision was made to build a new stadium within the walls of the old one.

Construction began in November that year, and the result is a unique-looking stadium inside the 'carcass' of the old, with bridges connecting the two. However, since not all the available space is utilised, the capacity of the stadium is now under half of what it used to be. Until FC Sachsen Leipzig climb the leagues, the stadium should be more than adequate.

RIGHT: A fine aerial view of Leipzig's Zentralstadion.

adidas
PHILIPS

Germany and Mexico battled for third place in the Confederations Cup at the Zentralstadion on 29 June 2005, the hosts running out 4–3 victors.

PLAK MEDIA
Tooor
SIEMENS

Continental
Fly Emirates
HYUNDAI
McDonald's
adidas
LEIPZIG
TOSHIBA
FUJIFILM
PHILIPS
AVAYA

1. FC Nürnberg (Nuremberg)

Stadium:	Frankenstadion
Address:	Max-Morlock-Platz 1, 90480 Nuremberg
Website:	www.fcn.de
Ground capacity:	45,000
Opening date:	1928, renovated in 1991 and then 2006
Architect:	Günther Wörrlein
Most important games:	World Cup 2006 venue
Memorable moments:	2005 Confederations Cup semi-final: Germany 2 Brazil 3, 25 June 2005

Nuremberg is known as a city lost in the middle ages with castles and gothic churches—but after its recent 56 million euro renovation, no one could say the same about the town's football stadium. The Frankenstadion, home to Bundesliga side 1.FC Nuremberg, is shaped like a giant elongated octagon and has been selected to host five games in the 2006 World Cup, including four group stage matches and a knockout round.

Among the changes made to the stadium with the World Cup in mind, the pitch has been lowered by almost two metres to give a better view of the playing surface to the fans, and the capacity has been increased by almost 6,000 seats by extending the south-west and north-west stands.

It's not just the town that's steeped in history either. Before World War Two the Municipal Stadium, as it was known then, was used as a marching ground for the Hitler Youth, with Hitler saying at the time, he wanted to 'look every one of his boys straight in the eye.' Since then, however, Nuremberg has tried to move away from that section of its past, with the Frankenstadion undergoing two renovations since. Upon its first in 1991 the stadium received its current name; a decade later a multi-purpose arena was built immediately next to it, the Nuremberg Arena, in keeping with the city's exceptional record for sport.

PAGE 62: A DFB Cup match between FC Sachsen Leipzig and Dynamo Dresden at the Zentralstadion in August 2005.

PAGE 63: The floodlights are switched on at the Zentralstadion, June 2005.

RIGHT: An aerial view of the Frankenstadion in Nuremberg in June 2005.

NÜRNBERG
TOSHIBA
FUJIFILM
PHILIPS
AVAYA
T-Mobile

HYUNDAI
10

Left: The 45,000-capacity Frankenstadion pictured before the gates are opened.

RIGHT: Panoramic view of the Frankenstadion, June 2005.

TOSHIBA
FUJIFILM
Bud
Bud
PHILIPS
Bud
Bud
T··Mobile·
AVAYA
Bud
Bud
NAILA/OFR.
HÖCHBERG 94
SINN
Fly Emirates
MasterCard
adidas

Schalke 04

Exterior view of Gelsenkirchen's Aufschalke Stadium.

INSET: Schalke 04 banners during the 2004/05 Champions League home match against FC Basel.

Stadium:	Arena Aufschalke—Veltins Arena
Address:	Ernst-Kuzorra-Weg 1, 45891 Gelsenkirchen
Website:	www.arena-aufschalke.de
Ground capacity:	61,000 (53,000 for European and international games)
Opening date:	August 2001
Architect:	HOK Sport
Nickname:	Die Knappen
Most important games:	2004 champions League final, World Cup 2006 Venue
Memorable moments:	German Championship victory. Schalke 04 3 HSV Hamburg 0, 1958

Having a brand new stadium right next to your old one, and the remains of your original ground still in existence illustrates how far Gelsenkirchen's Bundesliga side Schalke 04 have come since their 1924 foundation. They are lucky still to have a state of the art multi-purpose arena to play their matches in.

Hailed as 'a pilot project for the whole world', the Veltins Arena, named after a deal was struck with the German brewery, was opened in 2001 in a match against Borussia Dortmund. The stadium uses many impressive new technologies, including the chipcard payment system at the turnstiles which takes the place of conventional ticketing, and the use of the knappencard—the arena's own currency, as it were, on which money is stored to be taken off quickly and securely at the customer's consent when purchases are made.

The Veltins Arena's attempt to be at the forefront of technology was rewarded when it was chosen to host the 2004 Champions League final between FC Porto and AS Monaco. The stadium can hold both indoor and outdoor events due to its retractable roof, ensuring these can progress whatever the elements, and the ability of the pitch to slide in and out of the arena solves the problem of maintenance inside a domed stadium.

Schalke fans will be grateful for a new covered arena, after their old Parkstadion left them vulnerable to the weather with only one side covered. But Schalke were no strangers to innovative technology when they arrived at their new home. The pitch at the old ground was some way below ground level, so the team used to have an elevator to get them to and from the dressing room. Perhaps the strangest and most popular feature among thirsty fans who visit the new arena is the 5km pipeline that supplies the stadium with beer—helpful when demand is high, for example at a rock concert.

Schalker Fan-Club
S
04
Verband e.V.

BELOW: Schalke's ground, also known as the Veltins Arena, pictured before a game against Borussia Dortmund, with sponsor advertising prominent.

PAGE 74–75: An empty Aufschalke awaits opponents Borussia Dortmund.

RIGHT: Opening night for the new Aufschalke Stadium, 13 August 2001.

0:0
BVB
PHILIPS
adidas

Rheinfels
Rheinfels Quelle
Rheinfels
VICTORIA
FC SCHALK
VELTINS
erdgas
VELTINS

VELTINS
Pattex
THOMASBERG
NEU BECKUM
WINKELS
www.apa.de

VfB Stuttgart

Stadium:	Gottlieb-Daimler-Stadion
Formerly:	Neckarstadion
Address:	Mercedessrasse 87, 70372 Stuttgart
Website:	www.vfb-stuttgart.de
Ground capacity:	57,000
Opening date:	26 July 1933
Architect:	Paul Bonatz
Most important games:	World Cup 2006 Venue
Memorable moments:	VfB Stuttgart 0 Chelsea 1 Champions League, 25 February 2004

The fourth largest of the 2006 World Cup stadiums, the Gottlieb-Daimler Stadium has hosted over 20 internationals featuring the German international team in the last 50 years in addition to group matches in the 1974 World Cup and the Italy versus USSR semi-final of the 1988 European Championships. Consequently we know exactly what to expect in the summer of 2006.

Sitting in the middle of the Cannstatter Wasen sports complex in Stuttgart and hailed in Germany as one of the most beautiful cities in the world, the stadium is the home of Bundesliga side VfB Stuttgart, who occasionally share with their rivals SV Stuttgarter Kickers. Though many of the 12 venues selected to host the World Cup this summer are being rebuilt to fit in with FIFA regulations, the Stuttgart arena complied as early as 2001 when they refurbished the stadium's main stand at a cost of 50 million euros.

That didn't, however, stop officials at the Gottlieb-Daimler putting the wheels in motion on a new modernisation programme in 2004. The main tasks involved technically improving the ground, including a redesign of the ticketing system, and adding a new deck to one of the stands. Also added were two video walls with a surface area of 115 square metres, giving fans video replays of anything they may have missed. In keeping with German culture, there will be a section for spectators to stand, a capacity of approximately 57,000 dropping to 54,000 when the arena becomes all-seater.

The Neckarstadion, as it was known until a name change in 1993, will hold a total of six matches in the summer tournament: its allocation of four group matches and two straight knockout games including the third place play-off indicates its stature, ranking just behind the Olympic Stadium in Berlin where the showcase final is to be held.

RIGHT: Stuttgart's Gottlieb-Daimler Stadium.

debitel debitel
ODDSET

The Gottlieb-Daimler Stadium during VFB Stuttgart's 0–0 draw with Werder Bremen in August 2001.

debitel debitel debitel

Above: Stuttgart hit the back of the net with their second goal of a 2–0 victory against Dortmund in October 2004.

Right: An aerial view of Stuttgart's home ground, October 2005.

Page 82–83: A panoramic view of the San Siro stadium in Milan during the Serie A match between AC Milan and Lazio, 6 February 2005.

KÄRCHER

SECTION 2: European Football Grounds

SONY SONY SONY
OPEL

AC Milan/Internazionale

Stadium:	Stadio Giuseppe Meazza
Address:	Via Piccolomini 5, 20151 Milan
Website:	www.acmilan.com, www.inter.it
Ground capacity:	85,700
Opening date:	Opened: 19 September 1926, renovated in 1950 and 1990
Nickname:	San Siro
Most important games:	World Cup 1990 venue
Memorable moments:	First match AC Milan 3 Internazionale 6

One of the biggest and best-known stadiums in the world, the San Siro Stadium in Milan is shared by the city's Serie A duo AC Milan and Internazionale, otherwise known as Inter Milan. The stadium was built in 1925 and even then could hold 35,000 people, including a respectable seating capacity of 20,000. It's fitting that the ground's first match was an AC versus Inter derby, with Inter coming out 3–6 victors, but they were visitors that day. They did not move into the San Siro until 1947, some 21 years after construction, after the city council bought the stadium from AC Milan.

It is clear that the stadium is an important part of the city as, by 1939, the stadium was fully encircled with a capacity of 50,000 people. In 1955, with both AC and Inter in residence, the stadium had a second tier of seating added, increasing the capacity of the stadium further. In 1980, the San Siro underwent a name change in memory of Giuseppe Meazza, a man who played for both teams but was a legend at Inter, who died a year previously. Former Italy manager Vittorio Pozza once said that 'having Giuseppe on your team was like starting the match one goal ahead!'

In preparation for the World Cup in Italy in 1990, the San Siro was extensively renovated, the biggest development being a third tier added around the stadium except for the East Stand. This tier was held up by 11 cylindrical concrete structures, that have become the main visual aspect of the ground, and are actually used as staircases to access the third tier. Spectators high up in the West Stand get a view of the whole of Milan, due to the absence of a third tier opposite.

The San Siro went on to host three matches in the World Cup, and with capacity now 85,000 so it was no surprise when FIFA awarded the stadium five stars. It has gone on to host eight European club cup finals (UEFA Cup and Champions League), including Inter's triumph over Benfica in front of their home fans in 1965.

INTER

ADRIANO FOREVER
RHO
MORATTI
CORDOBA
ADRIANO
ZANETTI
PIZARRO
MATRIX
TOLDO
BASSO VICENTINO
ROMAGNA
NERAZZURRA
S. ARCANGELO PZ
SOCIAL CLUB
New FordFocus
Heineken
PlayStation 2
MasterCard
adidas
SHARP
uefa.com

LEFT: The Inter and Rangers players wait for kick off in front of an empty San Siro prior to the Champions League match on 28 September 2005.

BELOW: Inter defend a Rangers corner.

PREVIOUS PAGE: The San Siro Stadium, home of the mighty Milan duo—Internazionale and AC Milan.

PREVIOUS PAGE, INSET: Because of a UEFA supporter ban there's only one flag in the empty San Siro during the Champions League match between Inter and Rangers.

Ajax Amsterdam

Stadium:	Amsterdam Arena
Address:	Arena Boulevard 29, 1100 AM Amsterdam
Website:	www.amsterdamarena.nl
Ground capacity:	51,000
Opening date:	14 April 1996
Architect:	Rob Schuurman and Sjoerd Soeters
Most important games:	Euro 2000 venue
Memorable moments:	First match: 14 August 1996: Ajax versus AC Milan

Home to fading European football power AFC Ajax, currently playing in the Dutch Eredivisie, the Amsterdam Arena is a stadium befitting its team's history. With a capacity of 51,000 and still under ten years old, it was the first European stadium to have a retractable roof upon completion in 1996 and was the first stadium in the world to have a main road running underneath it.

The stadium's roof is still the main feature. The two halves can normally be opened and closed in 30 minutes, although this can be achieved in as little as five minutes, should circumstances require. There are two tiers of seating running round the whole of the inside of the arena, uninterrupted on the top deck, and separated only by four exits on the bottom, ensuring the stadium empties safely and quickly.

There were originally plans for a running track around the pitch but this was scrapped after lack of public investment due to the imminent Gulf War. A 2,000-capacity car park lies directly beneath the controversial playing field, which is infamous in Holland for its poor quality and has been replaced over 30 times in its short lifespan. This is because of the lack of air and ventilation available; a contributing factor could be the one-metre squared tiles, known as 'terraplas', that are put over the grass when the arena hosts non-sporting events. The tiles are see-through and are said to be able to stay on for a maximum of five days without damaging the grass, though this is open to debate.

The Amsterdam Arena staged five matches during the 2000 European Championships, including a quarter-final and the semi-final between Italy and joint hosts Holland, with Italy triumphing 3–1 on penalties. It has also hosted the annual 'Amsterdam Tournament', a pre-season contest between four teams that pits Ajax against three major European teams, including at various times the Premiership trio of Liverpool, Manchester United and Arsenal.

AJAX

AMSTEL
Focus C-MAX
adidas.com
SHARP
uefa.com
SINCE 1976
UEFA CUP
AJAX
F-SIDE

LEFT: Ajax lose 0–1 to Juventus in the Champions League in September 2004.

BELOW: Ajax squaring off with Juventus again, this time in a Champions League Semi-Final in April 1997. Juve won 2–1.

PREVIOUS PAGE: A 1997 exterior view of the home of Ajax Amsterdam.

ABOVE: 'Visit the world of Ajax'— the entrance to the Ajax ground.

Anderlecht

Stadium:	Constant Vanden Stock Stadium
Address:	Theo Verbeecklaan 2, 1070 Bruxelles-Brussel
Website:	www.rsca.be
Ground capacity:	26,000
Opening date:	1918, renovated 1983
Architect:	Michael Boelens
Nickname:	Parc Astrid
Most important games:	Anderlecht 1–1 Tottenham Hotspur. UEFA Cup Final, first leg 9 May 1984
Memorable moments:	Anderlecht 3 Arsenal 1. Fairs Cup Final, first leg 22 April 1970

Sitting in the middle of Astrid Park in Brussels, the Constant Vanden Stock Stadium is home to Royal Sporting Club Anderlecht, who play in the top league of Belgium, the Jupiler League, and play regularly in Europe, including 20 seasons in the Champions League. It was first built in 1917 when it was called the Stade Emile Verse, in honour of a patron of the club, though in day to day use the stadium is commonly known as Parc Astrid.

Originally the ground only had one wooden stand so concrete stands were later constructed, but in 1983 the ground was completely rebuilt in five stages; each of the four stands was tackled systematically, and a completion period included the construction of a roof. The new stadium had a capacity of up to 29,000, reduced to some 26,000 in European competition when an all-seating format is required.

From the air the Constant Vanden Stock Stadium looks every bit a state of the art sporting venue, its rectangular shape clad with cantilever roofing. Inside are two tier stands all the way round. One of the most interesting points about the stadium, and the focus of it, is the way business seats, shielded by glass, run the length of the stand. These are basically armchairs to sit on. Behind these lounges and restaurants complete the executive experience. The business seats even have volume controls to regulate the crowd noise as it is broadcast through speakers. Business conferences are also held at the ground on non-matchdays using these facilities.

Upon its renovation in 1983, the new stadium was renamed in honour of a past player and club president for 15 years, Constant Vanden Stock; the position of club president is currently occupied by his son, Roger.

RIGHT: The Constant Vanden Stock Stadium on 21 February 2001 before Anderlecht's 1–4 loss to Leeds United.

PlayStation.2
EUROCARD
MasterCard
FORD
AMSTEL BEER
motogp
EUROCARD

ABOVE: Fans during the 30 September 2003 Champions League match between Anderlecht and Bayern Munich. The game ended 1–1.

RIGHT: Belgium's national stadium is the King Badouin Stadium seen here during a Belgium-Netherlands exhibition match in 2003.

BELGIUM
NETHERLANDS
1
1
JVC
BIG BOSS
NIKEFOOTBALL.COM

Arsenal

Stadium:	Emirates Stadium
Address:	Ashburton Grove, London
Website:	www.arsenal.com
Ground capacity:	60,000
Opening date:	August 2006
Architect:	HOK Sport, Venue and Event Architecture
Nickname:	Ashburton Grove
Most important games:	None to date
Memorable moments:	None to date

After nearly a century at Highbury, their home since 1913, Arsenal's plan to move 600 metres to a new stadium at nearby Ashburton Grove was a controversial one. The 60,000-capacity stadium was built by the company responsible for the Stade De France in Paris and boasted a similar roof design along with four tiered stands.

With matchday revenue of £28 million dwarfed by TV income of £52 million, mostly generated by participation in the Champions League, critics said the money would be better spent on the team, especially since a redeveloped Highbury would have a capacity not far short of 50,000. But since the Gunners failed to make a profit when they won the Double in 2002 they felt they had no long-term option but to relocate.

The move from Highbury was first announced by Arsenal in November 1999 and was originally scheduled for August 2005, but in the event was postponed a year. Funding for the stadium project was problematic, but construction work finally began at the new stadium site in early 2004. Highbury itself would be redeveloped for housing, the four stands being used to house around 450 flats and the pitch remaining as a communal garden for their residents.

Naming rights of the Ashburton Grove stadium were granted to the Emirates airline, but the financial impact was still a worry to fans. Director Keith Edelman claimed the multi-million-pound loan Arsenal took out to fund the stadium would be spread over 25 years and would not impinge on the playing budget. The increase in gate capacity from 38,000 to 60,000 would see it support nearly 50 percent of the club's income, increasing matchday earnings by about £20m a season and reducing reliance on Champions League and broadcasting revenues. Arsenal's players reverted to the 'redcurrant' kit worn for the first season at Highbury for their last there before relocation.

RIGHT: Highbury Stadium was the home of Arsenal FC from 1913. It also saw 12 internationals—mainly friendlies.

ENAL STADIUM

LEFT: Many people will miss the relaxed atmosphere of Highbury and its leafy Islington surroundings when the club moves to Ashburton Grove.

RIGHT: Highbury's Clock End during the April 2003 Premiership 2–2 draw against Manchester United.

mobile.com
ANGELS
Chrysalis
LONDON EXPORT
IGUANA
ICAP
SPORTS NETWORK
NORWICH UNION
GB LITHO
Apax
JVC
Lloyds TSB
defy limits
BARCLAYS
plaza Restaurants
Subbuteo

FC Barcelona

Stadium:	Nou Estadi Del Futbol Club Barcelona
AKA:	Nou Camp
Address:	Avinguda Aristides Maillol, 08028, Barcelona
Website:	www.fcbarcelona.com
Ground capacity:	98,800
Opening date:	24 September 1957, renovated 1980, and 1994
Architect:	Francesc Mitjans Miró and Josep Soteras Mauri
Most important games:	World Cup 1982 Venue
Memorable moments:	First match: Barcelona 4 Warsaw 2

At a staggering 48 metres high, the Camp Nou in Barcelona is outwardly as intimidating as the Spanish giants who play there. FC Barcelona eventually moved into the Nou Estadi Del Futbol Club Barcelona—the stadium's official name—in 1957, although the plans to move there were created some nine years earlier.

The arrival of Hungarian Ladislau Kubala in 1950 seemed to signal to everyone the end of Barca's old Les Corts Stadium, as it was just too small, even with a 60,000 capacity. Debates over the site of the new stadium hampered its progress, but a change in club president in February 1954 ensured the first brick of the Nou Camp was laid just a month later.

The ground's first major reconstruction occurred when 22,000 extra seats were added to the third tier in preparation for the 1982 World Cup; this raised the stadium's overall capacity to 115,000. The Nou Camp went on to host five matches in the tournament, including the opening ceremony and a semi-final between eventual would champions Italy and Poland. A decade later the Olympic games came to Spain and the stadium held the final of the football tournament, where the hosts Spain won gold against the Poles, who must by now have been thinking the Camp Nou was not their lucky ground.

As well as several footballing events, concerts have been held at the arena by the likes of Bruce Springsteen, Michael Jackson and Pavarotti. The stadium seems to be in continuous development, to keep up with FIFA and UEFA regulations. The scoreboards have been changed three times, each time incorporating new technology, and the light, sound and media facilities are always being improved.

The summer of 1994 saw the pitch lowered by almost three metres and the lower tiers increased—factors which paid off four years later when UEFA awarded the stadium 5-star status. Barcelona wasted no time in making use of this by hosting the final Champions League final of the last millennium, where Manchester United stunned Bayern Munich to snatch the silverware in stoppage time.

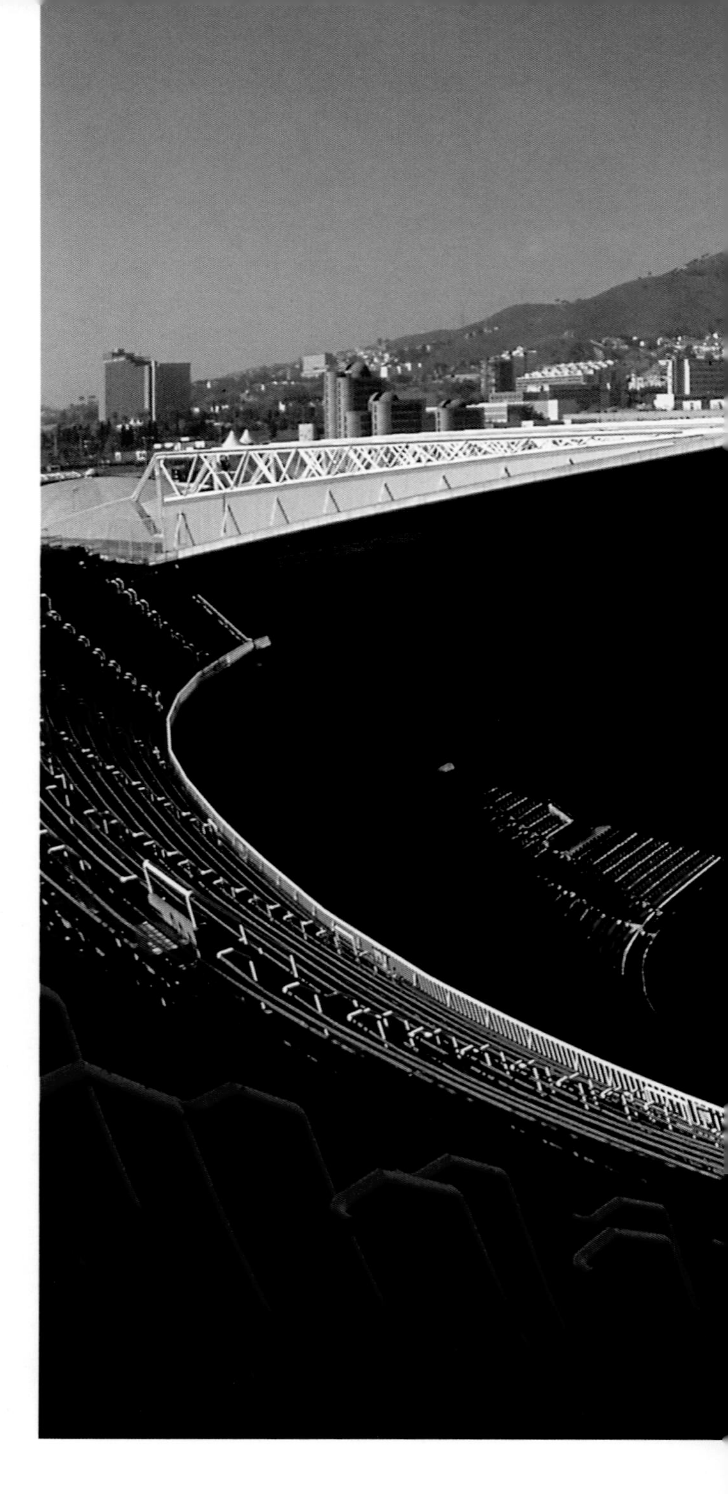

Left: View from the halfway line of the Nou Camp.

Above: The calm before the storm—Barcelona prepare to play Seville during the 2003/04 season.

Previous page: One of the world's great stadiums: a 2001 view of Barcelona's Nou Camp.

FC Basel

Stadium:	St Jakob Park
Address:	St. Jakob-Strasse 395, 4052 Basel
Website:	www.baselunited.ch
Ground capacity:	33,433
Opening date:	1954, renovated 2001
Architect:	Herzog & De Meuron
Most important games:	Switzerland–West Germany 25 April 1954

The St Jakob Park is Switzerland's first multi-purpose stadium and one of the most beautiful venues in Europe. In its original form it opened in April 1954, the year in which Switzerland (FIFA's home country) became the first European postwar hosts of the World Cup, and was inaugurated with a match pitting the home country against that tournament's eventual winners, West Germany.

It was built on the south-eastern edge of the city in extensive parkland, and during the competition hosted some memorable games, including England's 4–4 draw against Belgium and West Germany's 6–1 semi-final demolition of Austria, a fixture that filled the stadium to 58,000 capacity. (Basel is in Switzerland's German-speaking region.) After the World Cup it became home to the city's foremost club, FC Basel (established 1893).

Reopened in 2001 after a remarkably short rebuilding period of two and half years, its bold architecture and ultramodern structure makes the new St Jakob Park an imposing sight. Indoor and outdoor events held here include not only national and international football matches, but rock concerts, exhibitions and shows. The final touch is added by a fitness centre and a 33-outlet shopping centre.

Two large digital screens entertain fans sitting in the blue and red seats finished in the colours of FC Basel. The stadium's current capacity of nearly 33,500 includes 9,000 standing places.

A fascinating but little-known fact is the fact that the inclined south-facing roof covering the north stand incorporates solar panels, visible only from the executive boxes opposite, whose annual electricity production is more than is required to illuminate all football matches held during the year. The St Jakob Stadium can thus justifiably claim to be one of the greenest sporting venues in the world—and not just in terms of the playing surface.

RIGHT: The Basel and Manchester United teams exchange handshakes before the start of their Champions League match.

INSET: Swiss fans wave flags during their successful 2–0 European Championship qualifying match against the Republic of Ireland at Basel in October 2003.

VERON
4
SOLSKJAER
20
TOYOTA
BROWN
24
O' SHEA
22
P. NEVILLE
3
SCHOLES
18
10
BARTHEZ
1
AMSTE

SL Benfica

Stadium:	Estadio Da Luz
AKA:	Estadio Do Sport Lisboa e Benfica
Address:	Av. General Norton De Matos 1500, Lisboa
Website:	www.slbenfica.pt
Ground capacity:	65,000
Opening date:	25 October 2003
Architect:	Damon Lavelle
Nickname:	Cathedral of Emotions
Most important games:	Final venue of Euro 2004
Memorable moments:	First match: Benfica 2 Nacional Montevideo 1

Certified as the largest stadium in Portugal, Estadio Da Luz in Lisbon is home to the biggest club in Portugal, two-times Champions League winners SL Benfica. Translated into English, the ground's name means Stadium of Light, an appellation Premier League side Sunderland used for the ground which replaced Roker Park. It was also the same name of Benfica's previous ground, which got the name from the local neighbourhood.

The first stadium still had a healthy capacity of 80,000 even when it was made all-seater, but was technically inferior and the seats were uncovered. The new stadium was built right next to its predecessor, even overlapping it in places. It has been designated a 5-star stadium by UEFA and now is much more than a football stadium. It houses a gym, swimming pool, restaurants, and an amusement centre among other things, ensuring it isn't just used on match days.

The stadium's transparent roof and sloping, continuous upper tier allow the maximum amount of light into the ground, intensifying the bright red seats and justifying the stadium's name. The main reason for the construction of a new stadium was the European Championships of 2004, held in Portugal. Consequently the 'Cathedral of Emotions' hosted five matches in the tournament, including three England matches against France, Croatia, and Portugal.

The biggest event in the ground's short history is undoubtedly the Final, where underdogs Greece overcame hosts Portugal. With the stadium and its name inextricably intertwined, rumours of a possible naming deal with electronics company LG or mobile phone giants Samsung are worrying traditionalists, but nothing has come to fruition.

RIGHT: The Estadio da Luz in Lisbon. The 65,000-seater stadium was the largest during Euro 2004 and hosted the 4 July final between hosts Portugal and shock winners Greece.

Left: The Estadio da Luz is an impressive sight from the air.

Above: The Estadio da Luz pictured during the final of Euro 2004.

Brondby

Stadium:	Brondby Stadion
Address:	Brøndby Stadion 30, 2605 Brøndby
Website:	www.brondby-if.dk
Ground capacity:	29,000
Opening date:	1965, renovated 1998-2000
Most important games:	Brondby IF 2 Bayern Munich 1 Champions League, 16 September 1998
Memorable moments:	Record attendance attained 18 June 2003 against FC Copenhagen—31,508

The Brondby Stadion in Brondby, Denmark is over 40 years old, but it took almost that long to resemble a stadium of any kind. Home to Danish Premiership side and Champions League participants Brondby IF, the foundations for the ground were first laid in 1965—but with the stadium standing at an unbelievable 50 centimetres tall, it resembled a field rather than a professional football ground. Thirteen years later, in 1978 the ground's first stand was erected, followed closely by floodlights. This enabled evening and night matches to be played, essential if the club was to compete in Europe.

It progressed further in 1982, a year after the club turned semi-professional, housing 5,000 more spectators opposite the existing stand. In 1985 Brondby became Denmark's first fully professional football team after they won their first league championship in the top division. The two stands were covered five years later with the construction of roofs, but it was only in 1992 that it began looking like a stadium of any description; the addition of stands behind both goals 28 years after its inauguration increased the ground's capacity to 20,000.

In 2000 Brondby IF purchased the ground from the council and invested £20 million in virtually rebuilding it, joining all four stands and raising the capacity to nearly 30,000 for domestic matches. The front facade has a corporate look about it, like many British grounds, while in order to keep passion alive in the stadium, the lower tiers behind the goals are terraced for domestic fixtures and converted to seating for Europe.

Above: Interior view of Brondby's ground during training.

Right: A fine aerial view of the Brondby Stadium.

Chelsea

Stadium:	Stamford Bridge
Address:	Fulham Road, London, SW6 1HS
Website:	www.chelseafc.com
Ground capacity:	42,500
Opening date:	1877
Architect:	Archibald Leitch
Most important games:	Chelsea 1 Charlton 0 FA Premier League. 7 May 2005 (Chelsea presented with first title for 50 years)
Memorable moments:	Record Attendance: 82,905—Chelsea–Arsenal 1935

Now home to one of the 'Big Three', boasting a wealth of household and international names and an unlimited transfer war chest, it is hard to imagine that a team playing at Stamford Bridge could ever be in debt and playing at an unfinished stadium for a period of time. In fact, this was a comparatively recent situation.

Stamford Bridge was opened in 1877, but it wasn't until the turn of last century that it was considered for football use. It was offered to Fulham but they rejected the proposal, so it was given to Chelsea in 1904. Chelsea soon entered the league and Stamford Bridge hosted three FA Cup Finals from 1920 to 1922.

The construction of a new North Stand was halted by the Second World War in 1939 and it would be over 25 years until Stamford Bridge would undergo its first major changes.

The West Stand terrace was redeveloped to include seating, reducing the capacity of the stand by almost 60 percent from 20,000 to 6,300; this was increased to 13,000 in 2001. The Stadium's East Stand was next on the reconstruction list in the 1970s but was not finished until 1991 because of Chelsea's extreme financial hardships at the time. In the end it became a mammoth three-tiered stand. The construction of a new South Stand was completed in 2001, complete with a hotel and restaurant complex, known as Chelsea village, the intention being that Stamford Bridge didn't have to survive solely on footballing revenue. With the arrival of Russian multi-millionaire Roman Abramovich, the point now seems somewhat irrelevant.

RIGHT: Stamford Bridge hosting the Premiership match between Chelsea and Charlton, May 2005.

BLUES NEWS 0906 600 7760
BLUES NEWS 0906 600 7760
Orange
SIEMENS mobile
Fly Emirates
Fly Emirates
SANYO
OWERDAY
Fly Emirates
Fly Emirates
www.chelseafc.com
chelseafc.com

ABOVE: Poor attendance at Stamford Bridge during a cold January 2002 FA Cup third round replay match between Chelsea and Norwich City. Blues fans were cheered up by a 4–0 victory.

RIGHT: A 1997 view of Stamford Bridge—the pre-Abramovich days.

AUTOGLASS
SANYO
EURODOLLAR
UMBRO
Ladbrokes
ABBEYGATE

Club Brugge (Bruges) KV/Cercle Brugge KSV

Stadium:	Jan Breydel Stadion
Formerly:	Olympiastadion
Address:	Olympialaan 74, 8200 Brugge
Website:	www.clubbrugge.be
Ground capacity:	29,000
Opening date:	1975, renovated 1999
Most important games:	Euro 2000 Venue
Memorable moments:	Belgian Cup final. Cercle versus Club, 1986

The Jan Breydel Stadium has only recently been renamed, formerly answering to the rather bland and familiar name of the Olympiastadion. It is shared by Belgian Jupiler League duo Club Brugge KV, and their underachieving younger rival Cercle Brugge KSV.

While sharing the same home ground, efforts have been made to ensure the two clubs coexist peacefully. The Club Brugge fans occupy the south end of the ground behind the goal at the so-called Bad End, while the Cercle fans are situated opposite in the Kerk End. When, in 1986, the clubs met in the Belgian Cup Final, they fought it out at the Olympiastadion instead of at Heysel, where such finals are traditionally held. Club Brugge ran out predictable winners.

It would be two more years before Cercle beat their rivals on home soil—in November 1988, an epic 13 years after the ground opened. A decade before the all-Brugge cup final, the Olympiastadion hosted a UEFA Cup final, second leg, when Club drew 1–1 with giants Liverpool, but it wasn't enough to overcome the Reds' 3–2 first leg advantage. They would meet again two years later at Wembley Stadium in the European Cup Final, where Liverpool edged a 1–0 win.

The Olympiastadion underwent extensive renovation in 1999, with the capacity being increased by 12,000 and bringing the stadium in line with UEFA regulations. This was all in preparation for the European Championships, jointly hosted by Belgium and the Netherlands a year later. In the process it also underwent a name change, being named after a medieval rebel leader from Flanders. Now with its own identity, the Jan Breydel held three group games and a high-profile quarter-final between Spain and eventual winners France.

RIGHT: Panoramic view of the Jan Breydel Stadium, one of the venues for Euro 2000.

ABOVE: Karel Poborsky of the Czech Republic scores from the penalty spot during the European Championship 2000 group stage against France. It would prove futile as France won 2–1.

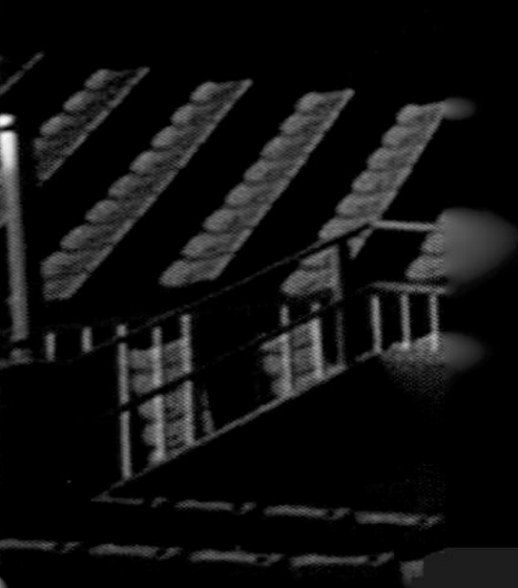

RIGHT: Another view of the impressive Jan Breydel Stadium.

JAN BREYDEL
STADION
PROXIMUS
PROXIMUS
PROXIMUS
PROXIMUS

CSKA Moskva/Dynamo Moscow

Stadium:	Dynamo Stadion
Address:	36, Leningradsky Prospect, Moscow 125190
Website:	www.cska-football.ru
Ground capacity:	37,000
Opening date:	19 May 1928
Architect:	Alexander Langman and Leonid Cherikover
Most important games:	Hosted football tournament in the Olympics 1980
Memorable moments:	First Match: FC Dinamo 3 RKimA 2

The largest stadium in Russia until the opening of the Lenin Stadium in 1956, the Dynamo Stadium in Moscow—not to be confused with the stadiums in Tbilisi or Minsk of the same popular name—is home to both CSKA Moscow and Dynamo Moscow.

CSKA, or the Central Army Sports Club as it's officially known, became the first Russian team to win a European club cup competition in 2005 when they upset Portuguese giants Sporting Lisbon at their own stadium in the the UEFA Cup. They then lost out in the Super Cup, falling to Champions League winners Liverpool in August of the same year. They are considered by some to be the Russian equivalent of Chelsea as they have a deal with oil company Sibneft owned by billionaire Chelsea owner Roman Abramovich, though the deal is nowhere near as lucrative.

Hardly Stamford Bridge, the totally uncovered bowl-like stadium is characterised by its dominating leaning floodlights, symbolic of the two club's pasts—rooted in the police and military forces. In 1938, a subway station, named Dynamo Station, was built near the ground, and the stadium was revamped for the 1980 Olympics held in Moscow.

During the Olympics the stadium hosted football matches, the highlight being the third place play-off between the host nation and Yugoslavia, the USSR winning by a single goal. It wasn't until 1998 that the wooden benches for fans were replaced by plastic seats, giving the stadium a capacity of 37,000 people—quite different to the days when its 60,000 could be stretched by another 10,000 if necessary—in the days before rules for international competition were as stringent as today.

RIGHT: CSKA Moscow players celebrate with the trophy at the end of the UEFA cup final against Sporting Lisbon, 18 May 2005. Moscow won 3–1.

FAR RIGHT: Liverpool train in Dynamo Stadium prior to a game against Spartak Moscow.

Ford
AMSTEL BEER

Deportivo la Coruna

Stadium:	Estadio Municipal De Riazor
Address:	Manuel Murguía 15011 La Coruña
Website:	www.canaldeportivo.com
Ground capacity:	34,600
Opening date:	28 October 1944, renovated 1982, 1995
Architect:	Michael Boelens
Nickname:	Ramon del Llano
Most important games:	World Cup 1982 Venue
Memorable moments:	First Match: Deportivo 2 Valencia 3

The tale of Deportivo la Coruna's Estadio Riazor is one of a club constantly swimming against the tide. When opened in 1944, the stadium had a capacity of 45,000 places and was inaugurated in October in a match against Valencia which was lost 3–2 in front of only 18,000 spectators. To add to the misery of the opening day, the first goal scored at the ground was by a Valencia player.

Things went from bad to worse when Depor were relegated in their first season at the Riazor, named after the nearby beach, amid complaints about the stadium and rumours that the pitch was possessed by the devil. The club went on to yo-yo between the top two divisions for the next few decades until, in the early 1980s, the then Second Division club redeveloped the Riazor for the World Cup.

Plastic seats with backs replaced cement benches and, while the stadium grew in comfort, it decreased in capacity by 10,000. The Riazor went on to host three group stage matches at the World Cup, Madrid and Barcelona dividing the showpiece fixtures between them. A deal was struck a year later between the town mayor and the club, allowing Depor to have a lease of the stadium for 50 years, paying just one peseta per year as a symbolic gesture.

In the 1990s things started to look up as Depor found success on both the domestic and European stages and changes to the stadium were made. The stands were brought closer to the pitch and cover was erected, though unpopular features like the metal crush fences remained. The new version of the Riazor opened in 1998, but some fans were unhappy with the all-seater layout and, in the first two games after the stadium's re-inauguration, some 200 seats were ripped out and stolen.

Technical developments were made in 2000 in preparation for Depor's foray into the Champions League, and there have been ambitious plans to built a new stadium with one end open to the sea. Lack of funds have meant the plan has yet to come into fruition, however.

Focus C-MAX
MasterCard
uefa.com
FUSILIERS

PREVIOUS PAGE: **The Estadio Municipal de Riazor pictured during the UEFA Champions League match between Deportivo la Coruna and Liverpool in November 2004.**

PREVIOUS PAGE, INSET: **PSV Eindhoven players during their training session at the Riazor Stadium in September 2003, before a clash with Deportivo.**

RIGHT: **Deportivo beating Hamburg 2-1 at the Riazor during the 2000 Champions League.**

AGUILA-AMSTEL
MOTO RACER WORLD TOUR
FORD

Dynamo Kiev

Stadium:	Stadion Valeriy Lobanovskyi
Address:	Grushevski Str.3 UKR-252 001, Kiev-001 Ukraine
Website:	www.fcdynamo.kiev.ua
Ground capacity:	83,200
Opening date:	1934
Architect:	Grechina
Most important games:	Dynamo Kiev 3 Bayern Munich 3. Champions League Semi-Final. April 7, 1999
Memorable moments:	22 October 1997 Dynamo 3-Barcelona 0. (Kiev won 4–0 at the Nou Camp weeks later)

Formed in 1927, Dynamo Kiev is the main professional football club in the Ukrainian capital of and, though founded as an amateur team, later became officially funded by the Soviet state. This led to players from the 1950s to the 1980s enjoying the status of police officers. Dynamo was bought from the state in 1993 by Hryhoriy Surkis, a Jewish/Ukrainian businessmen who is one of the richest tycoons in Eastern Europe with interests in electricity and oil.

The club has consistently rivalled Moscow's giants in the domestic league and in the 1970s–1980s provided the majority of the Soviet Union's national team. Kiev won the Cup Winners' Cup in 1975 and 198, reaching the semi-finals of the Champions League in 1999.When the Soviet Union collapsed, the club became a member of the new national football league, which they proceeded to dominate under the Ukrainian name of Dynamo Kyiv. They won nine consecutive Vyscha Liha (Ukraine Premiership) titles between 1993 and 2002 until they were finally toppled by major rivals Shakhtar Donetsk who emerged from the country's eastern region. They relegated Kiev to second place again in 2005.

The stadium was named in honour of a former Kiev and national team coach who died in 2002 after a heart attack that occurred during a game. Valeriy Lobanovskyi was also at one time coach of the USSR national team. (The Ukraine have played international games here.)

The ground that carries his name is a big blue oval bowl, is situated in a picturesque park located in the centre of the city, close to the Dnipro River. The stands behind the goal are quite a long way from the pitch, but those alongside the pitch are as close as would be expected

The club also has a modern training base in the suburb of Koncha-Zaspa and has a renowned youth coaching system which has produced such prodigies as Andriy Shevchenko.

Domestic games are played at the Lobanovskyi but big European games take place at the 90,000-capacity Olimpiyskiy Stadion, formerly the Respublikansky, which is part of the city's National Olympic Complex.

LEFT: Kiev's players celebrate with the trophy after their final match against Shakhtar Donetsk on 29 May 2005. Dynamo took the Cup of Ukraine for the seventh time.

ABOVE: Supporters of Dynamo Kiev protest in front of the government building in Kiev, in March 2005 after a Kiev court had frozen shares in the club when a senior minister warned the club could be targeted in a probe into past privatisations.

Everton

Stadium:	Goodison Park
Address:	Goodison Road, Liverpool, L4 4EL
Website:	www.evertonfc.com
Ground capacity:	40,2000
Opening date:	1892
Architect:	Archibald Leitch
Nickname:	The Grand Old Lady
Most important games:	First match: Everton 4 Bolton 2
Memorable moments:	Record attendance 78,299: Everton versus Liverpool, September 1948

Erected just across Stanley Park from Anfield, Goodison Park, home of Everton Football Club, is a ground of many firsts and records. Hailed as the country's first major football stadium in 1892, it became the first ground to employ under-soil heating, the first ground to have a reigning monarch to visit it as King George V did in 1913, and it holds the record of hosting more England Internationals than any other English club ground.

Such was the stadium's capabilities that it wasn't until the turn of last century that it started developing further, with a two-tiered stand built on the Park End, and the construction of the main stand on Goodison Road. In 1926 another stand was built opposite the main one, while in the 1930s Everton introduced the concept of the dug-out to England after seeing it employed at Aberdeen's Pittodrie ground.

In 1938 a fourth double-tiered stand was built at Goodison, the first one of its kind in the country. Almost 30 years later five games of the 1966 World Cup were held at Goodison Park, the second highest amount of games held in any one place in the tournament. These included a quarter-final. Five years later, the Main Stand was demolished and a new stand, twice the size and with three tiers, was put in place, with floodlights lining the gantries.

There would then be a gap of over 20 years before any major new developments when the new Stanley Park End stand was rebuilt in 1994 in the wake of the Taylor Report. Everton's ground could now accommodate a total of 40,200 fans on matchdays, nearly half their record attendance when terraces were the norm. Still, Goodison remained the club's beloved home and, with a potential joint stadium with Liverpool a non-starter, and financial constraints holding back attempted relocation to a dockside site, it looks likely to stay that way.

RIGHT: Goodison Park pictured in August 2002 before a match against Tottenham Hotspur.

THANKS FOR YOUR GREAT SUPPORT
KEJIAN 科健
Bluepride
alder travel
CLIMAX SCAFFOLDING LTD
"WE PRACTICE SAFE ACCESS"
JAGUAR
JAGUAR
DAVID McLEAN
ANC MERSEYSIDE
KILBRIDE

EVERTON 2
WOLVES 0
4:23 28:26

Left: Everton beat Wolverhampton Wanderers 2–0 at Goodison in November 2003.

Right: The home of the 'Toffees'.

Fenerbahçe

Stadium:	Sukru Saracoglu Stadyumu
Address:	Fenerbahçe Tesisleri, Kadikoy, Istanbul
Website:	www.fenerbahce.org
Ground capacity:	52,000
Opening date:	1908, renovated 1999
Nickname:	Kadykoy
Most important games:	Euro 2004 qualifier—Turkey 0 England 0, October 2003
Memorable moments:	Fenerbahçe 3 Manchester United 0. Champions League. 8 December 2004

Istanbul's Fenerbahçe are a team that pride themselves on being the best in Turkey, and they have a stadium to match in the Sukru Saracoglu. Opened in 1909, it was known as the Priest's Marsh due to the conditions surrounding the ground.

The stadium was bought outright by Fenerbahçe in 1933, thanks to the efforts of club President Sukru Saracoglu, who was also Turkey's finance minister at the time. A new stadium with a capacity of 25,000 was built In the 1940s, but was deemed too small and, in a 1962 deal which sold the stadium back to the government, Fenerbahçe were promised a new stadium with a capacity of 40,000 within four years. While building was occurring, the team played at neighbours Besiktas' Inonu Stadium, but were not to move back into their own stadium until 21 years later.

However, while at Inonu, the club's success on the pitch wasn't affected as they won eight championships during their exile. What's more, they completed a domestic league and cup double just two years after their return in 1983. The stadium's capacity was reduced to 21,000 when it went all-seater in the 1990s, so construction of a new Sukru Saracoglu Stadium began in 1999. It was a purpose-built football stadium, with no running track round the perimeter—a first in Turkey—with a maximum capacity of 60,000 spectators but, in typical Fenerbahçe style, construction wasn't quick.

Each stand was individually demolished and rebuilt, ensuring that Fenerbahçe didn't have to endure any more time away from their home, but it wasn't until the beginning of the 2005–06 season that work was finally completed. The stadium was also the scene for the highly unsavoury Euro 2004 qualifying match between Turkey and England in October 2003.

Right: Fenerbahçe and Schalke enter the Sukru Saracoglu Stadium before their Champions League match in October 2005.

Right: The Fenerbahçe fans reveal a banner before the game against Schalke.

NO COMMENT
NO COMMENT
UNITE AGAINST RACISM
avea
VICTORIA

Ferencvaros Torna Club

Stadium:	Ulloi Ut
Address:	1091 Budapest IX, Ülloi út 129
Website:	www.ferencvaros.hu
Ground capacity:	18,100
Opening date:	19 May 1974
Most important games:	FTC 3 Millwall 1. UEFA Cup. 30 September 2004
Memorable moments:	First game: Ferencvaros 0 Vasas 1

Quite a modest football stadium at first sight, the Ulloi Ut Stadium in Budapest, Hungary, is home to Ferencvaros Torna Club, who play regularly in Europe. Unfortunately, the club are more known as much for their unruly fans than they are for their exploits on the pitch, a Millwall fan being stabbed when the sides met in the UEFA Cup in 2004.

The stadium is named after a highway which runs past the North Stand, and holds 18,000 spectators. That capacity is significantly reduced from the 38,000 for which it was licensed in the 1940s, and this is due to an incident that occurred in the Ulloi Ut in 1947. Sections of the ground's wooden stands collapsed during an international match when Hungary hosted Austria due to the mass of spectators being too heavy. It emerged afterwards that tickets had been touted and more fans got in than should have, sending them hurtling towards the ground below.

Surprisingly, no one was killed in the incident and perhaps even more surprising is the fact the match carried on. The ground was shut down and it would be some 27 years before Ferencvaros returned to their home to find it all-seater and with a diminished capacity of 18,100. The stands are open, with no roof.

The most unusual part of the stadium is to be found outside the clubhouse and behind one of the goals. The statue of a naked man commemorates a Dr Ferenc Springer, the club's founder in 1899.

Right: A 2004 view of the Ulloi Ut before a Ferencvaros-Sparta Prague match.

ABOVE: Hungary's national stadium is the Ferenc Szusza. Accompanied by his teammate Roland Juhasz (left) and Bulgarian Dimitar Barbatov (right), Hungarian Adam Komlosi heads the ball during a 2006 World Cup qualification match.

Feyenoord

Stadium:	The Feyenoord Stadium
AKA:	De Kuip
Address:	Van Zandvlietplein 3, 3077 AA Rotterdam
Website:	www.feyenoord.nl
Ground capacity:	51,100
Opening date:	27 March 1937, renovated 1994
Architect:	Brinkman and van de Vlugt
Most important games:	Euro 2000 Venue
Memorable moments:	First match Feyenoord 5 versus Beerschot 2

The Feyenoord Stadium, known internationally as simply 'De Kuip' (the Tub), was one built before its time. Club President Leen van Zandvliet had a dream of a stadium with no obstructions of the pitch, and one which would keep all the noise inside, creating an intimidating atmosphere. The stadium has since been used as a blueprint for grounds like the Nou Camp.

Since opening in 1937, De Kuip has hardly known a dull moment. It holds the record for staging European club competition finals, including Aston Villa's only European Cup victory against Bayern Munich in 1982, and the Champions League final of 1972, where Feyenoord's compatriots Ajax defeated Inter Milan.

The undoubted highlight for the fans of the Tub came in 2002 when Feyenoord lifted the most recent of their 'magic ten' trophies, when the home side defeated Borussia Dortmund by three goals to two to lift the UEFA Cup. On top of that, the Feyenoord stadium has played host to over 150 international matches featuring the Dutch national side, including the 2–0 victory in October 1993 which virtually ended England's hopes of qualifying for the 1994 World Cup. The stadium's crowning glory came in 2000 when it hosted five matches in the European Championships, including a quarter-final and the showpiece Final between Italy and France.

Concerts by some of the biggest names in music have also been held in Rotterdam, including the likes of Michael Jackson, Guns N'Roses, and U2. In 1994 the stadium underwent renovation, including erecting a roof around the perimeter that covers the whole of the top tier and 80 percent of the stadium in total, and the ground was made in a 51,000-capacity all-seater stadium. A further building was constructed next to de Kuip, for commercial use by the club, containing a megastore, restaurant and club museum.

RIGHT: A general view of the De Kuip Stadium in Rotterdam.

VASTGOED
Schalke 04
FORTIS
BURGER KING
CANAL+
FORTIS
DOE LAND
ROBE DI KAPPA
BELKIN

LEFT: Feyenoord fans celebrate the 2–1 Champions League victory over Schalke in December 2004.

ABOVE: Another view of De Kuip Stadium before a Champions League match against Marseille.

PAGE 140–141: Fans in the Ali Sami Yen Stadium five hours before the kick off for the Galatasaray-Manchester United Champions League match in Istanbul, September 1994.

PAGE 140–141, INSET: Galatasaray supporters are known for their fanaticism.

Galatasaray

Stadium:	Ali Sami Yen Stadium
Address:	Mecidiyekoy, Istanbul
Website:	www.galatasaray.org
Ground capacity:	22,100
Opening date:	14 December 1964
Nickname:	Hell
Most important games:	Turkey v Bulgaria. International, December 1964
Memorable moments:	First Match: Turkey v Bulgaria, December 1964

The Ali Sami Yen Stadium is yet another stadium in the Turkish capital of Istanbul, and is home to Galatasaray SK. It is essentially a large oval concrete bowl, uncovered except for the length of the pitch. Even then the roofs only protect the upper tiers of seating, while floodlights weren't installed until the 1990s.

There is a running track surrounding the pitch, as there are many sections within the Galatasaray sports club, thought football is the predominant sport. The ground was named after one of the founders of the club, Ali Sami Yen, and the bright yellow and red seats proudly show the team's colours.

Controversy is never too far away from the stadium known affectionately as 'Hell' by the fans. In its very first match, an international between Turkey and Bulgaria, the stadium achieved a record attendance figure which has never been surpassed because it was overcrowded. When a small fire occurred in one of the catering stands, panic ensued and fans ended up being crushed. From then on a smaller limit was placed on the stadium.

Trouble reared its head again in April 2000 when two Leeds United fans were killed during crowd trouble outside the ground before a UEFA Cup semi-final. Galatasaray eventually won the cup, but it was overshadowed by these events, for which four men were arrested. The nickname 'Hell' comes from Galatasaray's fans, who use a variety of props including drums, torches, flares and flags to create a visual spectacle, particularly in European matches. Intimidating the opposition appears to work as Galatasaray have scalped many a European giant, including Barcelona, Real Madrid, and AC Milan.

Due to the deteriorating condition of the Ali Sami Yen, Gala played at the Ataturk Olimpiyat Stadium in Istanbul—the venue for the 2005 Champions League final—in 2003–04, but moved back the following season. Now they are building a new 41,000 seater stadium scheduled to open in 2007.

AR ÖLÜR GALAT SARAYLILIK ÖLME

Glasgow Celtic FC

Stadium:	Celtic Park
Formerly:	Parkhead
Address:	18 Kerrydale St, Glasgow, G40 3RE
Website:	www.celticfc.co.uk
Ground capacity:	60,000
Opening date:	1892, renovated 1994
Architect:	Archibald Leitch
Nickname:	Paradise
Most important games:	Celtic 3 VfB Stuttgart 1. UEFA Cup Quarter-final, first leg. 20 February 2003
Memorable moments:	Record attendance: 92,000 Celtic v Rangers, 1938

Visible from miles away, Celtic Park is home to former European champions Glasgow Celtic FC, who have dominated Scottish football, along with Old Firm partner Glasgow Rangers, for decades. Nicknamed 'Paradise', the ground is over a century old, although it has been modernised along the way while Celtic chase the dream of a ground worthy of its monicker.

In 1994 Celtic were ready to move to a new-purpose built stadium elsewhere in the city, but businessman Fergus McCann had other ideas which he began implementing when he bought the club in 1994. This resulted in three-quarters of the ground having two tiers and being supported by cantilever roofing. The North Stand has extra support in the form of concrete poles, so as not to encroach on the graveyard behind,. When finished, the 22,500 seater stand was unmissable, even from the air, with 'Celtic' blazed across the seats in white.

The South Stand is a listed building, with the front facade attached, so it was not totally redeveloped apart from a new transparent roof. Even though it already had two tiers, it was dwarfed by the new North Stand, giving the stadium a rather unbalanced look; the lower tier on the opposite North Stand is roughly as big as the entire South. With all the work finished, Celtic boasts the second largest football club ground in the UK, behind Old Trafford, and after a few more technical redevelopments, including work on the stadium's medical department, it will join neighbours Ibrox in being awarded the maximum five stars by UEFA.

PREVIOUS PAGE: A general view of the Ataturk Olympic Stadium during the Turkish Cup Final between Galatasaray and Fenerbahçe, 11 May 2005.

RIGHT: Celtic Park taken before the Old Firm match against Rangers in March 2003. Celtic beat their old rivals 1-0.

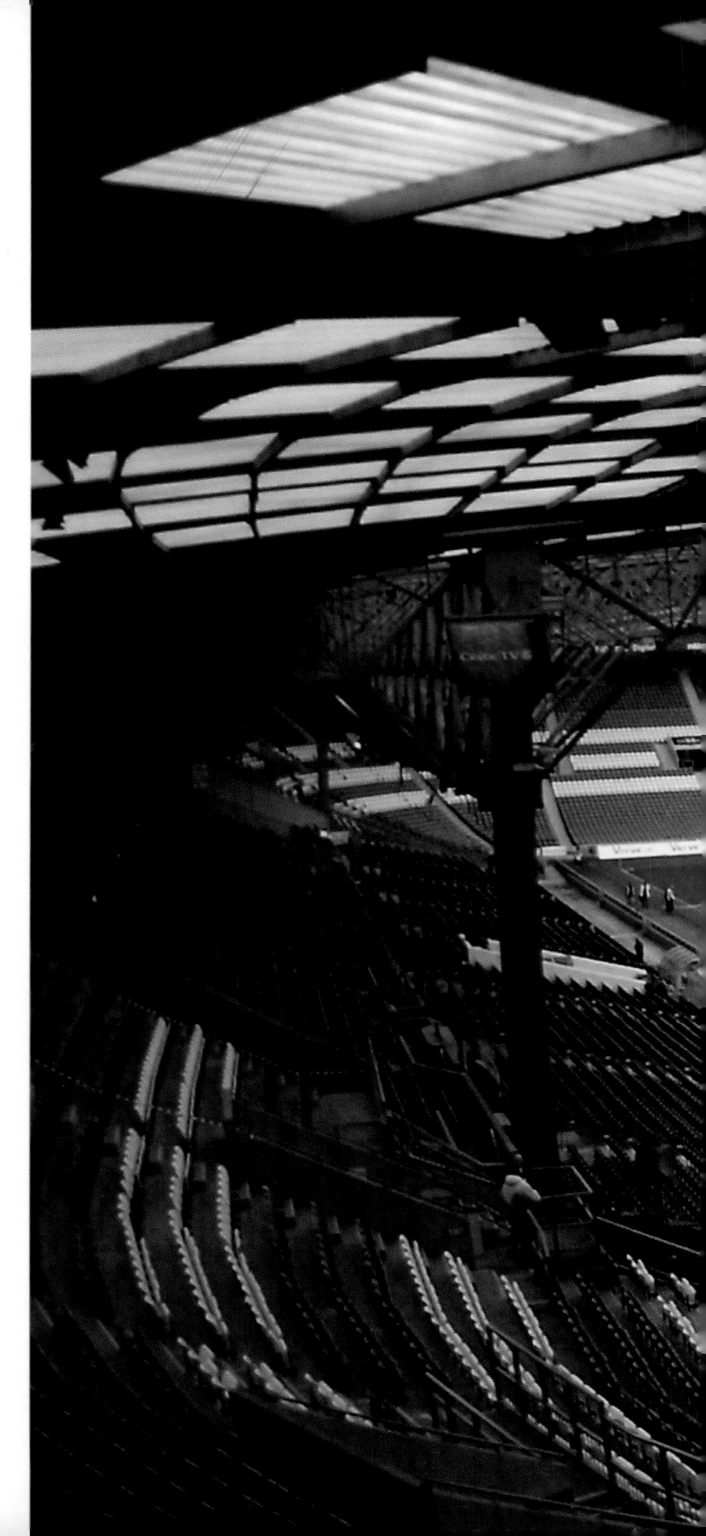

centralcarauctions.co.uk
PHOENIX HONDA
PHOENIX HONDA
FORREST
CELTIC
PHOENIX HONDA

LEFT AND ABOVE: Two more views of Celtic Park, one of the three major Glasgow stadia, alongside Ibrox and the Scottish national stadium at Hampden.

Glasgow Rangers

Stadium:	Ibrox Stadium
Address:	Edmiston Drive 150, Glasgow G51 2XD
Website:	www.rangers.co.uk
Ground capacity:	50,400
Opening date:	30 December 1899
Architect:	Archibald Leitch
Most important games:	First Match: Rangers 3 Hearts 1
Memorable moments:	Record attendance: 118,567 Rangers-Celtic, 2 January 1939

The Ibrox Stadium in Glasgow is part of the UEFA 5-star club, and has been at the forefront of stadium design and redevelopment in Britain for many decades. The current incarnation of Ibrox mixes state-of-the-art with tradition, with the red-bricked facade at the front of the stadium, designed by football architect Archibald Leitch in 1929, a listed building.

Home to Scottish Premier League side Glasgow Rangers, the stadium has suffered disasters over the years, these prompting the early developments. In 1902 Ibrox hosted an England versus Scotland international, but tragedy struck when the wooden terracing collapsed and killed 26 spectators. As a result the wooden terracing was scrapped at the order of Leitch, who was brought in, and it was replaced with solid earth foundations.

The capacity at Ibrox was still immense, as was proven with a British attendance record set in the traditional New Year's Old Firm derby, where Rangers and Celtic battled it out in front of 118,000 fans in 1939. The ground was left largely untouched for the 30 years after that game until disaster struck again at Ibrox. This time 66 people were killed through crushing and suffocation the same Rangers-Celtic fixture. This latest tragedy started the ball rolling for Ranger's home to become an all-seater stadium. In the decade following the second Ibrox disaster, £10 million was invested in redevelopment, with the construction of three new stands; the Broomloan, Govan and Copland. As a result, Ibrox lost its distinctive oval shape and adopted a more rectangular one.

Rangers' Chairman David Murray spent £52 million redeveloping the stadium in the 1980s and early 1990s, creating an all-seater stadium in 1991, some five years before most other top flight clubs fell into line.

RIGHT: A pitch-level view of a Scottish Premier Division match between Rangers and Celtic at Ibrox Stadium. Rangers won the match 4–0.

1873
RANGERS F.C.
1873
MULTI METALS
NORTHERN STEEL
STOCK
Nss

RANGERS F.C.
1873
adidas
SHARP
Focus C-MAX
AMSTEL
PlayStation.2
MasterCard
AMSTEL
PlayStation.2

OPPOSITE: Fans are left in no doubt whose stadium they're in.

LEFT AND BELOW: Ibrox exterior with (inset) the John Greig statue. Edinburgh-born Greig played a total of 877 games for Rangers and scored 120 goals. He was captain of Rangers when they beat Dynamo Moscow in the final of the European Cup Winners Cup in 1972 in Barcelona. He also won 44 Scotland caps.

Hajduk Split

Stadium:	Poljud Stadion
Address:	Poljudsko setaliste bb 21000 Split
Website:	www.hnkhajduk.hr
Ground capacity:	35,000
Opening date:	1979
Architect:	Prof. Boris Magas.Ph.D.
Nickname:	The Gradski Stadion
Most important games:	1979 Mediterranean games
Memorable moments:	Hajduk Split v Red Star (abandoned) Death of Josip Broz Tito 4 May 1980

The impressive Poljud Stadion in Split is home to Croatian side HNK Hajduk Split, but was originally built for the VIIIth Mediterranean Games in 1979, and was opened by Josip Broz, the then President of Yugoslavia better known as Tito.

There are only two main stands opposite each other, with transparent roofs, and are curved to give the stadium an attractive 'sea-shell' appearance. There is standing in the North Stand, and a scoreboard on the south side. As Split have ventured into the UEFA Cup and Champions League, the ground has entertained teams from around the world, and the Poljud Stadion has become on of the most intimidating grounds in the world, not least because of Hajduk Split's supporters, known as the Torcida.

Named after the group of Brazilian fans also known as the Torcida—from the Portuguese 'torcer', to cheer on—they are officially described as 'loyal and rowdy', and certainly give football in Croatia a South American flavour. However on one occasion when the team were on a bad run of form, a number of these fervent Split fans broke into the Poljud Stadion and dug eleven graves on the pitch—a warning to the team if they didn't improve.

Perhaps the most poignant and memorable moment at the Poljud stadium comes in 1980 when Tito died. Hajduk's president announced the news over the stadium's PA system, in the middle of a match between Split and Red Star from Serbia. The 50,000 crowd in attendance wept, as did players from both sides. A number collapsed on the floor, and the match was promptly abandoned.

RIGHT: Hajduk Split's Poljud Stadium pictured in February 2004.

FAN CLUB NATIONALMANNSCHAFT
www.dfb.de
FÜR EUCH !
FAN CLUB NATIONALMANNSCHAFT
www.dfb.de
FAN-CORNER
www.dfb.de
FAN-CORNER
www.dfb.de

HJK Helsinki

Stadium:	Finnair Stadion
Address:	Urheilukatu 1, 00250 Helsinki
Website:	www.finnairstadium.fi
Ground capacity:	10,800
Opening date:	2000
Architect:	Ritva Kokkola-Lemarchand and Olivier Lemarchand
Most important games:	FIFA under-17 World Championships. August 2003
Memorable moments:	FC Hämeenlinna 1 MyPa 2. Finnish FA Cup final. 1 November 2004

One of the most impressive stadiums in Europe—but in miniature form. That description sums up the Finnair Stadium in Helsinki. Sponsored by national airline Finnair, the stadium holds only 10,800 people. Tenants HJK Helsinki, by far the largest club in Finland and regular participants in the UEFA Champions League, took up occupation in June 2000, leaving the nearby Olympiastadion. Unusually this was deemed to large for them, due to the lack of football interest in Finland compared with the immense popularity of ice hockey.

The Finnair stadium was the first purpose-built football stadium in the country. Its most telling feature is its roof structure—the roof on the main side juts out like a claw above the rest, allowing two tiers of seating. As well as football, the Finnair Stadium has ventured into hosting music concerts, Tina Turner performing in late 2000, just after its inauguration. The Finnish national team have played at the stadium, and it also hosted the FIFA under-17 World Championships.

In May 2003, an artificial pitch was added to the stadium, and it was touted as a tool that would allow more youngsters to get into the game. The theory was that it would help Finnish football, as the country's harsh winters mean the game can really only be played in the summer months. But FC HJK, and particularly their English manager Keith Armstrong, didn't see the innovation as such a good thing. He said the pitch wasn't suitable for HJK's 'high tempo' style of football, saying 'because it doesn't give way, it's usually the player's ankle that does.'

Ironically, after moving because their old ground was too large, a Champions League clash against Israel's Maccabi Tel-Aviv was relocated to the nearby Pohjola Stadium to meet UEFA regulations.

RIGHT: The Finnair Stadium in 2000.

FAR RIGHT: Juho Makela of HJK (front) on his way to goal against Glentoran during the first round of Champions League qualifiers, July 2003.

elisa
elisa
HELSINGIN SANOMAT
Tänään täällä. Huomenna Hesarissa.
HELSINGIN SANOMAT
TOYOTA
Kauppalehti
Forza

Juventus

Stadium:	Stadio Delle Alpi
Address:	Str. Altessano 131, 10151 Torino
Website:	www.juventus.it
Ground capacity:	71,000
Opening date:	1990
Architect:	Hutter & Cordero
Nickname:	The stadium with no soul
Most important games:	World Cup 1990 Venue
Memorable moments:	First match: Juventus/Torino XI 4 Porto 3

An extremely impressive stadium visually, and the scene of England's crushing semi-final defeat to West Germany in 1990, the Stadio Delle Alpi has come under immense criticism over the last 15 years. It was built specifically for the World Cup in question, and clubs Juventus and Torino, who play in Serie A and B respectively, left their ageing Stadio Comunale home, excited at the prospect of a 71,000 seater stadium named Delle Alpi because of Turin's close proximity to the Italian Alps.

Since then however, the ground has become known as 'the stadium without a soul' by fans, who miss their old home with all its history, and do not like its replacement, citing its location on the outskirts of Turin as one of the problems. The biggest problem, however, is the stadium itself. The running track surrounding the playing field is so immense that the fans are a long away from the action—particularly behind the goals, where the fans are almost half a pitch away. As a result it is very hard to create an atmosphere.

Touted as having a capacity of 71,000, factors such as having to separate home and away fans, and the fact that a complete view of the pitch cannot be obtained from the lower seats, reduce the Stadio Delle Alpi's useable capacity to some 10,000 less than the advertised figure. The fans hold the stadium in contempt and are not afraid to tell people about it, with the result that Juventus, a club known the world over, has suffered some embarrassing moments. In the 2001–02 season in a Coppa Italia match against unfashionable Sampdoria, only 237 spectators showed up—less than 1 percent of the stadium's capacity.

In the summer of 2003, Juventus bought the stadium and immediately set about plans to rebuild it in the same location. Torino have purchased the old Stadio Comunale, and will move into a new stadium on that site in 2006. Amongst the rebuilding, Juve's new ground will have a halved capacity of about 35–40,000 and will be modelled after English stadiums by removing the running track. They also hope to follow Eindhoven's example of creating a venue that is utilised 365 days a year, with offices, restaurants, and a megastore among the features planned. Juventus have also struck a deal with LA-based company Envision for the naming rights to the new stadium.

RIGHT: Juventus fans crowd the Delle Alpi pitch during the Serie A match against Atalanta, June 2001.

Visteon
O DINO

LE·GRU
UN OCEANO DI PASSIONE IN UN MARE
FIAT STILO
pensare avanti
GIRLS

LEFT: General View of the Delle Alpi Stadium during a league match between Torino and Juventus, February 2002.

BELOW: With the stands of the Delle Alpi towering behind him, Alessandro Del Piero holds the Scudetto aloft at the end of the last Serie A match of the season against Cagliari, May 2005.

Lazio/Roma

Stadium:	Stadio Olimpico
Address:	Via Foro Italico, 00194 Roma
Website:	www.asromacalcio.it www.sslazio.it
Ground capacity:	82,000
Opening date:	1952
Architect:	Enrico Del Debbio
Most important games:	World Cup 1990 venue
Memorable moments:	Roma 1 Liverpool 1 (Liverpool win 4–2 on pens) European Cup final. 30 May 1984

Jewel in the crown of the FIGC (Italian FA), the Stadio Olimpico in Rome is another in a long list of Olympic Stadiums across the world, and unsurprisingly, was built with the 1960 Olympic Games firmly in mind. Its circular construction is unmissable, and it is the home to Serie A duo SS Lazio, and AS Roma, who both moved from the U-shaped Flaminio Stadium, site of Italy's World Cup triumph over Czechoslovakia in 1934.

The home of the Roma fans is the south stand, known as the Curva Sud, while the Lazio fans congregate opposite in the Curva Nord. 30 years after the Olympics, the Stadio Olympico was allocated four games of the 1990 World Cup, its hosting of the showpiece final between West Germany and Argentina cementing its place as the best stadium in the country. In recent years that title has been strongly contested, due to the continuous development of Milan's San Siro stadium.

The Stadio Olimpico has been awarded the coveted UEFA 5-star stamp of approval, and has hosted three Champions League finals. Roma were inspired in 1984, reaching the final in front of their own fans, but failed to make the most of their home advantage, falling 4–2 on penalties to Liverpool. The Merseysiders were no strangers to cup finals at the Olympico, winning another of their famous European five titles seven years earlier at the stadium. Seven years after their final defeat, Roma beat Internazionale 1–0 in an all-Italian UEFA Cup final second leg, but it was not enough as Inter had done the damage earlier with a 2–0 victory at the San Siro. Once again, the supporters in the Curva Sud had to watch another team lift the silverware.

RIGHT: Roma play Lazio at the Olympic Stadium, 29 April 2001.

PAGE 162: An empty Stadio Olimpico during a Champion's League match between AS Roma and Real Madrid in December 2004. Roma were forced to play the match behind closed doors due to crowd problems.

PAGE 163: The Olympic Stadium during the UEFA Champions League match between AS Roma and Leverkusen in November 2004.

AS Roma
0
CHAMPIONS LEAGUE
Real Madrid CF
0
SHARP
Ford
Focus C-MAX
Ford
AMSTEL

SEMPREFORZAROMA
UNICO GRANDE AMORE
Focus C-MAX
BIRRA MORETTI
PlayStation.2
MasterCard
AMSTEL
SHARP

Legia Warsaw

Stadium:	Stadion Wojska Polskiego
AKA:	Stadion Legia
Address:	Ul. Laziengkowska 3, Warszawa
Website:	www.legia.com.pl
Ground capacity:	15,400
Opening date:	1930
Architect:	Aleksander Kodelski and Maksymilian Dudryk-Darlewsk
Most important games:	First post-war Polish international: July 1947 Poland vs Romania
Memorable moments:	First Match: Legia 1 Barcelona 1. 9 September 1930

The idea for a stadium for Polish side Legia Warsaw was first mooted in 1920, when the club settled. However, due to constant financial restraints it took a decade for the finishing touches to be added and for the ground to be completed.

After drawing cash from various sources, largely donations, Legia's first ground opened its doors for a match against WisBa in October 1922 which ended in defeat for Legia. The problem of cash flow still floated over the club so the solution was found in Legia selling the site to the army, in return for the money to complete the stadium.

Legia also received the rights to play at the ground and in 1925 the ground was ready for use, but more trouble followed. Later that year another army-governed club, Lechia Warsaw, was allowed to share the ground with Legia, and with backing of influential army members, tried to evict Legia altogether. A brief squabble ensued, after which the military powers-that-be awarded Legia sole tenancy: they have stayed at the Stadion Wojska Polskiego ever since.

Officials at Legia then appealed to the Bank Gospodarstwa Krajowego for the funds to finally finish the sporting venue, and were given as injection that proved sufficient to complete the ground in 1930. Its facilities also included a running track, cycle track, a new covered stand and some 10 tennis courts. When the Second World War arrived, the stadium was taken over by the Nazis and used as an artillery post, with trenches dug in the pitch; fortunately, no serious damage resulted from this occupation. Floodlights were added in 1960, and, while the stadium can accommodate Legia's average gate, plans are now in hand for the club to rebuild and modernise the Stadion Wojska Polskiego once again.

RIGHT AND PAGE 166: An empty Legia Stadium basking in Polish sunlight prepares for the European Championship qualifier between Poland and England, 1999.

LEGIA
YORK
AGFA
Auchan

AGFA
Auchan
GATE
WAY

Liverpool

Stadium:	Anfield
Address:	Anfield Road, Liverpool, L4 OTH
Website:	www.liverpoolfc.tv
Ground capacity:	45,000
Opening date:	1884
Architect:	Archibald Leitch
Most important games:	First International game—England versus Ireland 1889
Memorable moments:	Russia 3 Czech Republic 3. Euro 96. 16 June 1996

There's no doubt that Anfield is one of, if not the, most famous football grounds in England. It's a ground steeped in history, as reminders of the club's history are visible all around the stadium, from the Shankly gates and Paisley Gateway to the tributes for the Hillsborough and Heysel disasters. Even when the players are in the tunnel, poised to enter the field of play in front of 45,000 supporters, the simple sign stating 'This is Anfield' says all it needs to say.

Ironically, it was close neighbours Everton who began life at Anfield, until a dispute over rent with its owner, brewer John Houlding, resulted with them moving across Stanley Park to Goodison, where they still reside today. Houlding was left with a stadium that he had poured money into, including the erection of an 8,000-capacity stand, so he made the business decision to create a new team to use the ground. That team was Liverpool FC.

They played their first game at Anfield in 1892 with a 7–1 win over Rotherham. The Kemlyn Road Stand was constructed on the current site of the main stand and the Anfield Road Stand was built in 1903, followed three years later by perhaps the most famous stand in football—the Spion Kop. A journalist from local newspaper the Liverpool Echo suggested the name, after a hill in South Africa—the site of a battle in the Boer war that left many dead, many with strong ties to Liverpool. Once extended and covered in 1928, the Kop held some 30,000 people, more than some whole football stadiums.

The Anfield Road terrace was converted to all-seating in 1983 and nine years later in 1992, a second tier was added to the Kemlyn Road Stand, which was rechristened the Centenary Stand in celebration of 100 years of Liverpool and, consequently, Anfield. This now housed 12,000 spectators. After the Hillsborough disaster of 1989, the Taylor Report obliged all stadia in the top two divisions to become all-seater, so the Kop was remodelled in 1994. It became a 12,500 all-seater stand that kept the same name and is still the focal point of Anfield's vocal support.

A pre-season friendly between Liverpool and Parma at Anfield. The home side triumphed 5–0.

BELOW: The Kop is a sea of colour before the Champions League quarter-final between Liverpool and Bayer Leverkusen in April 2002.

RIGHT: Another full-house at Anfield to watch the European Champions.

www.liverpoolfc.net
RADIO CITY 96.7
Reebok
adidas
PlayStation
liverpoolfc.net

Maccabi/Hapoel Tel-Aviv

Stadium:	Blumfield Stadium
Address:	Behind Jerusalem Boulevard in Jaffa, Israel
Website:	www.maccabi-tlv.co.il
Ground capacity:	16,500
Opening date:	1962
Architect:	Archibald Leitch
Memorable moments:	Maccabi 2 Hapoel 0. Israel League, 18 September 2005

Situated on Jerusalem Boulevard, just down the road from the local McDonalds, a footballing ground like the Blumfield Stadium is hardly what you would usually find in Israel, but is indicative of global westernisation. Even the name doesn't fit, unless its history is understood. The stadium was named after a rich Jewish businessman called Bernard Blumfield who donated a lot of money to Israel. Incidentally Bernard's brother Louis was accused of organising the assassination of former US President John F. Kennedy.

Home to Israel Premier League sides Maccabi and Hapoel Tel-Aviv, two of Israel's most famous teams, who together make up almost half of the Israeli National team. Maccabi pay their big European matches at the nearby Ramat Gan national stadium, where they used to play all their home games. Also a few games in the winter are played there while repairs are made to the playing surface. Maccabi won a championship title in 2003 in Ramat Gan stadium after opponents Hapoel Petach Tikva switched the venue in order to gain more gate receipts. In 1968 Maccabi's Chairman, Geri Beit Halevi suggested they move in with neighbours Hapoel, and has proved to be of financial benefit since. The ground is totally uncovered and the colour-co-ordinated seats are split red/black and yellow/blue, representing both its home teams, and were installed in 2000. Maccabi are celebrating their centenary in 2006—however, the Blumfield Stadium almost didn't make it that far when in September 2004, suicide bomber Mohammed El-Ghazi was caught. He confessed he planned to detonate at the ground a few days later. In recent months the ground has been improved further, through updating the toilets and installing a car park.

RIGHT: One of Hapoel Tel Aviv happiest memories—supporters celebrate beating Chelsea 3–1 on aggregate in the 2001 UEFA Cup.

FAR RIGHT: Security is always an issue today. Republic of Ireland's Robbie Keane passes an Israeli police woman following a training session at the Blumfield Stadium, 24 March 2005.

Maccabi Tel Aviv play their European matches at the larger Ramat Gan national stadium.

MasterCard
PlayStation 2
AMSTEL
AMSTEL
Focus C-MA
PlayStation 2

Malmo

Stadium:	Malmo Stadion
Address:	Kulan, Eric Persson vag, Malmo Stadion
Website:	www.mff.se
Ground capacity:	26,500
Opening date:	1958
Architect:	Fritz Jaenecke and Sten Samuelson
Most important games:	1958 World Cup Venue
Memorable moments:	Record attendance: 30,953 Argentina v Germany, 1958

Built for the staging of the World Cup by Sweden in 1958, the Malmo Stadium looks larger than the capacity suggests. This could be because of its bowl-like construction, with two narrow curved roofs running up either side and the ends remaining uncovered. Like most European sports clubs with footballing sections, the stadium has a running track surrounding the playing area, leaving the possibility of ground expansion by removing it should the need arise.

The area immediately surrounding the stadium is manufactured to be pleasing to the eye—the trees are planted in line, the grass perfectly cut. The World Cup proved to be particularly rewarding for Malmo, the stadium celebrating its record attendance—30,953 for the group match between West Germany and Argentina—which still stands today. At this point the stadium only had one stand.

The Malmo Stadium held three other World Cup matches, including a quarter-final where West Germany played at the ground again, this time overcoming a stubborn Yugoslavia. Aside from being built for an international competition, the stadium is also home to Swedish side Malmo FF, whose most notable European achievement came in 1979 when they reached the European Cup final before falling to Brian Clough's Nottingham Forest in the first half of their European Cup double.

The second roofed stand was added In preparation for the European Championships of 1992. England visited twice, though it hardly proved a lucky venue as they failed to score.

FAR LEFT: Sweden versus Switzerland, a friendly in front of nearly 20,000 spectators on 17 March 2002. The score was 1–1.

LEFT: Some 26,500 spectators watched Malmo play IFK Helsingborg on 19 June 2001.

BELOW: A panorama of Malmo stadium and its locality in 2003.

Manchester United

Stadium:	Old Trafford
Address:	Sir Matt Busby Way, Old Trafford, Manchester M16 ORA
Website:	www.manutd.com
Ground capacity:	68,000
Opening date:	1909
Architect:	Achibald Leitch
Nickname:	Theatre of Dreams
Most important games:	Highest attendance: 70,504 versus Aston Villa 1920
Memorable moments:	Semi-final at the European Championships of 1996 between France and Czech Republic (Czech Republic win 6–5 on penalties)

Home to arguably the biggest club the country has ever known and possibly the most famous stadium in Europe, Old Trafford was opened in February 1910 with just one stand, after the site had been acquired by brewer J H Davies a year earlier. It was bombed in the Second World War by the Germans and Manchester United had to temporarily play at Maine Road, home of neighbours Manchester City, until their return in 1949.

Nearly half a million pounds was spent on preparing Old Trafford as a World Cup venue in 1966, and by 1985, 75 percent of the ground was covered in a modern self-supporting cantilever roof which allowed spectators an unobstructed view of the pitch, free from supporting beams. Further developments meant that, by 1994, the Theatre of Dreams was an all-seater stadium but, with a capacity of just 44,000, it wasn't big enough. Action was taken and two years later in 1996 a three-tiered 26,000 capacity North Stand, bearing 'Manchester United' on the seats, was completed at a cost of £19 million. This stand also holds the United Museum and well-stocked trophy room.

Old Trafford hosted a semi-final at the European Championships of 1996. At the turn of the Millennium second tiers were added to both stands behind the goals, creating an even more intimidating Stretford End as a result. With a capacity of now 68,000, Old Trafford regularly hosts FA Cup semi-finals as a neutral venue, and in 2003 it hosted the all-Italian Champions League final between AC Milan and Juventus. Even with the largest capacity in English club football, the long-term plan is to rebuild the South Stand in the same image of the north, and to fill in all four corners, bringing the ultimate capacity up to 92,000 people.

RIGHT: The famous exterior façade of Old Trafford, with the statue of legendary United manager Matt Busby.

PAGE 180: A panoramic view of the interior of the Theatre of Dreams, November 2003.

HESTER UNITED

FEB 6TH 1958 THE FLOWERS OF MANCHESTER MUFC THE RELIGION
MANUTD.COM
PEPSI PEPSI
vodafone
MANUTD.COM

vodafone
vodafone
vodafone
vodafone
vodafone
vodafone
MANUTD.COM
MANUTD.COM
DIMENSION DATA MANUTD.COM

Another view of Old Trafford, with its 68,000 capacity

RIGHT: Old Trafford hosts Premiership newcomers Portsmouth, November 2003.

MANUTD.COM
vodafone
105·4
UNITED

MANUTD.COM
PEPSI
BARCLAYCARD
QUATTRO
The world's

AS Monaco

Stadium:	Stade Louis II
Address:	7, Avenue des Catelans, 98000 Monaco
Website:	www.asm-foot.mc
Ground capacity:	18,500
Opening date:	1985
Architect:	Henri Pottier
Most important games:	UEFA Super Cup Final Venue
Memorable moments:	Monaco 3 Chelsea 1. Champions League semi-final. 20 April 2004

It took 2004 Champions League finalists AS Monaco 15 years to find their home in the first Stade Louis II, but once there in 1939 they plied their trade in the French Ligue 1. Soon the club was attracting 33 per-cent of Monaco's 30,000 inhabitants each week for home games; the stadium needed to expand, but there was simply no room due to the high water level. So in the 1970s a 15-year programme was put into action to reclaim land through the application of dams and other tactics.

The dry land they reclaimed was named Fontvielle Village, and three hectares were allocated for a brand new stadium, work on which began in 1981. In January 1985 Prince Rainer, Louis II's grandson and heir, opened the second version, built to survive earthquakes up to 7.5 on the Richter scale due to the nature of the land it was built on.

The layout of the stadium is of particular interest. Inside is a car park, an Olympic-sized swimming pool and a in hall to be used for a wide range of sports—all underground! The ceiling of the car park is actually the foundations for the pitch. A striking feature of the stadium's architecture are the nine arches at the front of it, keeping with the theme of the Monarchy. Apart from letting the fans view the stunning views of the hills as well as the football, the winds coming off the hills also ventilate the pitch.

The Stade Louis II hosted five UEFA Super Cup Finals in a row, but with a capacity of just under 20,000 it will struggle to hold anything more prestigious.

RIGHT: Chelsea warm-up during a training session in April 2004 at Stade Louis II as they prepare to face Monaco in the Champions League semi-final.

PAGE 186: An evening football match at the Louis II Stadium in Monte Carlo, Monaco.

PAGE 187: A Monaco training session at the Louis II, on the eve of the UEFA Cup first round against Willem II, September 2005.

32
FEDCOM
21
FEDCOM
17
FEDCOM
FEDCOM
19
21

Olympiakos

Stadium:	Karaiskaki Stadium
Address:	Possidonos Avenue, Faliro-Athens
Website:	www.olympiakos.gr
Ground capacity:	33,300
Opening date:	June 2004
Architect:	Stelios Agiostratitis
Most important games:	2004 Olympic Games. Soccer Venue
Memorable moments:	Tragedy of Gate 7. 8 February 1981

Now in its third guise, the Karaiskaki Stadium in Piraeus, Greece was originally built in 1895 in preparation for the 1896 Olympic Games, and was originally known as the Velodrome because of its use as a multi-purpose sports venue.

In the 1920s it began to be used primarily for football, and became prominent in the domestic and international game, hosting the Greek national team on a number of occasions as well as being the venue for Greek FA Cup finals. It was reconstructed in 1964, and given its name after Georgios Karaiskaki, a general in the Greek revolution against the Turks in 1821 who died not far from the arena.

Once refurbished, the stadium continued to host high-calibre matches on the European stage; most notably, the Karaiskaki held the Cup Winner's Cup Final in 1971 between Chelsea and Real Madrid, and the replay two days later which the English club won. Tragedy struck in February 1981 when 21 Olympiakos fans died and tens more injured immediately after a 6–0 derby demolition of neighbours AEK Athens. The fans rushed towards the stadium's exits to celebrate with the team, but the turnstiles were still in place and the doors were almost shut, resulting in the fans being crushed and suffocating. Named the Victims of Gate 7, their seats at the Karaiskaki remain empty to this day.

In 2003, the stadium underwent its third and most recent transformation, being totally reconstructed for the 2004 Olympic Games. After agreeing to undertake the organisation and construction of the new stadium on the same site of the previous two in 2003, tenants Olympiakos were granted permission to use, but not own, the new Karaiskaki stadium until 2052. The stadium took as little as 14 months to build, and is identified by its 14 red pylons supporting the 33,000 seater stadium's roof, much like Dortmund's Westfalenstadion. The third incarnation of the Karaiskaki Stadium is also home to current European Champions Greece.

RIGHT: An aerial view shows the newly built Karaiskaki Stadium (right) and the Peace & Friendship closed stadium in Athens.

ATHENS 2004

LEFT: Members of the Costa Rican and Iraqi teams stand with the officials as their respective National Anthems are played during the Athens 2004 Olympic Games at Karaiskaki Stadium.

ABOVE: Olympic football: not always the most popular sport. Two fans take in the game between Italy and Paraguay during the Athens 2004 Olympic Games at the Karaiskaki.

Olympique de Marseille

Stadium:	Stade Velodrome
Address:	3, Boulevard Michelet, 13008 Marseille
Website:	www.om.net
Ground capacity:	60,000
Opening date:	13 June 1937, renovated: 1998
Architect:	Henri Ploquin
Most important games:	1938 & 1998 World Cup Venue
Memorable moments:	Brazil 1 Netherlands 1 (Brazil win 4–2 on penalties). World Cup 98 semi-final. 7 July 1998

With a capacity of 60,000 spectators, the Stade Velodrome is a magnificent edifice—but it almost was not built at all! Costs were perceived to be too high for construction in 1933, and the project was shelved. It was only when France got the nod for the 1938 World Cup that the decision was reconsidered and building resumed.

French Ligue 1 club Olympique de Marseille arrived in 1937 and has since graced it with top-flight football and frequent European competition. But the Velodrome is indelibly linked with competition on the world stage, namely the World Cup. It holds the distinction of hosting not one but two World Cup semi-finals, separated by 60 years and both featuring Brazil. In 1938 the Brazilians fell to Italy but were luckier against the Netherlands in the same venue half a century later, defeating them 4–2 on penalties before falling to hosts France in the final.

As well as two World Cups, Marseille's ground was also the setting for the legendary 1984 European Championship semi-final between France and Portugal where Michael Platini scored the winner in the last minute of extra time for the home side.

The stadium is interesting in the sense that only the Jean Bouin stand is covered, leaving the stands and the pitch exposed to the elements. Even after renovation in 1998 the stands were not covered, but a minimum capacity of 25,000 was assured at all times during the construction period. The Stade Velodrome is named after the tracks that surround the pitch, used for the running and cycling, and cycling events and tournaments that used to be held there.

RIGHT: The Velodrome pictured before the Champions League match between Marseille and Real Madrid, November 2003.

PAGE 198: Marseille enter the stadium before their fixture against Lyon at the Velodrome, August 2005.

PAGE 199: The Velodrome hosted the World Cup '98 clash between hosts France and Russia, with the eventual champions coming out 3–0 victors.

DROIT AU BUT
DROIT AU BUT
PlayStation.2
MasterCard
MasterCard
adidas
SHARP
uefa.com uefa.com

MARSEILLE
DODGER'S 92
n9uf
LG

anon
TIFO !
G-SHOCK

Olympique Lyonnaise

Stadium:	Stade Gerland
Address:	350 Avenue Jean-Jaures, 69007 Lyon
Website:	www.olweb.fr
Ground capacity:	42,000
Opening date:	1926, renovated 1982 and 1998
Architect:	Tony Garnier
Most important games:	2003 Confederations Cup Venue
Memorable moments:	Record attendance 48,552 Lyon–St-Etienne 1980

The Stade Gerland is without doubt a stadium that has stories to tell. Although its current occupants, frequent French Ligue 1 champions Olympique Lyonnaise, have been there since 1950, the stadium was used as a general athletics stadium for 20 years before that, construction having been completed by German POWs after the First World War in 1919.

Once Lyon had settled in, football gradually began to take precedence in the stadium, and in the early 1960s the cycle track surrounding the pitch that had held several Tour de France finishes, was destroyed as the football became more successful. At the latter end of the decade, the Roman-inspired four entrance gateways were named as historic monuments, and therefore could not be legally knocked down. In preparation for the 1984 European Championships, the Jean Jaurès and Jean Bouin stands were brought closer to the pitch, increasing capacity as a result.

The stadium underwent its second and most drastic renovation in time for the World Cup in 1998, where it was to host eight games in total, including a quarter-final between Germany and the tournament's surprise package Croatia. The two stands behind the goals were demolished and rebuilt, making the Stade de Gerland an all-seater stadium with a capacity of 42,000 people. Particular care is taken with the stadium's playing surface, which is never left to grow longer than 28mm and never cut shorter than 25mm. Tragedy struck the stadium in 2003 however, when a former Lyon player, Marc Vivien Foe, collapsed while representing Cameroon in the Confederations Cup semi-final against Colombia. He died later in hospital.

RIGHT: Olympique Lyonnaise fans anticipate their team's Champions League quarter-final clash against PSV Eindhoven, 2005.

HAUT LE CHEVRON DE LA
adidas.com
SHARP
uefa·com uefa·com

FAR LEFT: Lyon coach Paul Le Guen looks on as his team prepares to face Ajaccio, 2005.

LEFT: Lyon supporters known as the 'Bad Gones' add colour to their stadium, 2004.

Panathinaikos FC

Stadium:	Apostolos Nikolaidis Stadium
AKA:	Leoforos Stadium
Address:	Alexandras Avenue, Central Athens
Website:	www.pao.gr
Ground capacity:	17,000
Opening date:	1922, redeveloped 2001
Most important games:	Panathinaikos 2 Arsenal 2. Champions League. 21 October 2004
Memorable moments:	Record attendance against AEK Athens in 1963—26,126

The Apostolos Nikolaidis Stadium in Athens certainly sounds the part, but tenants Panathinaikos FC of the Greek First Division feel it doesn't look the part. They have been trying to secure planning for a new stadium for years, with little luck. However, they will probably have to look for another site on which to build their future, as the land that the stadium is built on belongs to the city of Athens. Panathinaikos were given 'free use' of the stadium, but the expiry date of 2012 creeps ever nearer.

The club moved from their home in 1984 to the Olympic Stadium in Athens, but returned 16 years later after renovations brought the stadium up to Champions League standards. The stadium was named after a deceased ex-club president, and is also known as the Leoforos Stadium, after its location in Alexandras Avenue, (Leoforos being 'avenue' in Greek). It has been home to several Greek footballing sides over the years, including Olympiakos and AEK Athens, and the Greek national side for a time.

Now distinguishable by the large, uncovered, sloping stands behind the goals, one with a giant clover displayed in white on the green seats, there's no doubt who plays there now. Under those stands lies a boxing ring, a swimming pool, basketball and volleyball courts, just some of the other sections of Panathinaikos sports club. The Leoforos was the scene of an amazing comeback in the Champions League of 2004–05. Panathinaikos were 3–1 down from the first leg against Polish side Wisla Krakow, with lucrative qualification for the group stages of the competition at stake. The home side managed to pull of a surprising 4–1 victory in front of their fans, with a 114th-minute winner, and ensured the ageing stadium would host yet more European football before the curtain fell.

RIGHT: Panathinaikos face Deportivo la Coruna at the Oaka Spiros Louis Stadium—Athens' Olympic Stadium—in season 2000/01.

PlayStation
FORD

Heineken
PlayStatio 2
CHAMPIONS LEAGUE
New FordFocus
Heineken

LEFT: A training session by Werder Bremen in September 2005 before their UEFA Champions League match against Panathinaikos at the Olympic Stadium.

Paris Saint Germain

Stadium:	Parc des Princes
Address:	24, rue du Commandant Guilbaud, 75016 Paris
Website:	www.psg.fr
Ground capacity:	49,000
Opening date:	4 June 1972
Architect:	Roger Taillibert
Most important games:	First Match: Marseille—Bastia 2–1
Memorable moments:	Liverpool 1 Real Madrid 0. European Cup final. 27 May 1981

The long-time crown jewel in France's crown of football stadia, the Parc des Princes was built by Roger Taillibert and was intended to host the Tour de France cycle race in 1897. It received its name after the land that it was built on, formerly a hunting ground for the Monarchy.

The Parc des Princes was essentially a velodrome (multi-sports facility) until 1937, when it became solely a football stadium. It was the first ground to host the European Cup Final as it was then known (now the Champions League) in 1951 and also used to be the home of the French national team until the creation of the Stade de France for the World Cup in 1998. While the French team moved across town to the new stadium, Ligue 1 and Champions League participants Paris Saint Germain stayed.

In the late 1960s a planned new ring road around the capital threatened the Parc des Princes, which was built in the way. A compromise was reached in 1970 when the whole ground was restructured so the road passed under one of the corners. The ground is identified by its 50 'ribs' along the perimeter which supports cantilever roofing, ensuring the two tiers of seating that run uninterrupted all around the elliptical arena all have a perfect view of the action.

PSG rely heavily on a deal with sporting company SESE for the stadium, that runs out in 2014, so the Parc des Princes is much more than a football stadium once again, with PSG's HQ, a giant megastore and a restaurant all included.

Right: An excellent aerial view of Parc des Princes with the Eiffel Tower (left) and Montparnasse Tower (right) standing out behind.

Page 210 and 211: Interior views of Parc des Princes — (211) before the 1998 World Cup match between Belgium and South Korea.

Final 98

LEFT AND BELOW: The Stade de France is situated to the north of Paris in the city of St.-Denis. The stadium, which can seat 80,000 people, opened its doors in January 1998, in time to host the World Cup. It is also a venue for track and field meets, rugby, concerts and other events.

Partizan Belgrade

Stadium:	Partizan Stadion
Formerly:	JNA Stadion
Address:	Humska 1, 11000 Beograd
Website:	www.partizan.co.yu
Ground capacity:	32,700
Opening date:	29 October 1949
Most important games:	Most important game Partizan v Red Star 14 October 2000 Match with bitter local rivals abandoned due to crowd rioting
Memorable moments:	First Match: Yugoslavia 1 France 1

The Partizan Stadium in Belgrade is home to 1966 European Cup finalists and many-times Yugoslavian Champions Partizan Belgrade. Built in 1949, its first match was an international between Yugoslavia and France, who battled out a 1–1 draw. This was a sign of the calibre of match that the stadium was to host in the future.

The ground used to be called the JNA Stadium, after the Yugoslav People's Army, but though it was later renamed many fans still refer to it under the original name. The stadium hosted many international matches until 1963 when rivals Red Star Belgrade had their ground renovated and took on the honour thanks to their improved facilities. The ground also hosts the Yugoslav Cup Final and, in the 1950s, it was even used as an outdoor cinema. Metallica also held a rock concert at the ground in 2004.

The stadium itself is a large uncovered bowl, as would be expected in its location. There is a large scoreboard in one of the stands, which is covered by yellow, blue and red seating, installed in 1998, with 'Partizan' emblazoned across them. As many sports are performed within the complex including the European Athletics championships of June 2002, there is a large running track surrounding the pitch.

Plans are currently being put in place for the construction of a new 45,000-seater stadium for the sports club, scheduled to open in 2007. The new and yet unnamed stadium is planned to have a retractable roof, allowing all-weather events, and is going to keep the running track around the playing surface.

RIGHT: Maccabi Petach Tikva's Toama Salim challenges Partizan Belgrade's Lomic Marko during their UEFA Cup first round match in September 2005 in Belgrade.

Below: In October 2005, Partizan supporters protested against the club management and decided not to cheer their club during a derby match against Red Star Belgrade. There were many empty seats.

FC Porto

Stadium:	Estadio Do Dragao
Address:	Avenida Fernao de Magalhaes, Porto
Website:	www.fcporto.pt
Ground capacity:	52,000
Opening date:	1962
Architect:	Manuel Salgado
Most important games:	Euro 2004 Venue
Memorable moments:	First match: FC Porto 2 Barcelona 0

Another UEFA approved 5-star product of Euro 2004, the Estadio Do Dragao is home to FC Porto, former UEFA Cup and Champions League winners. It is named after the presence of a dragon on FC Porto's crest, and Porto's fans are known as the Dragoes (the dragons). It was inaugurated in 2003 with a 2–0 victory for the home team over Barcelona, cementing the club's intentions for the new stadium after leaving the Estadio das Antas. Porto played their last match at their old ground in January 2004, and demolition began two months later.

The new 98 million euro stadium is a seven-day a week business, with conference centres, leisure facilities and restaurants; a residential area is planned for the future. The arena's main feature is the roof, named 'the veil' due to its transparency, which fills the stadium with natural light. Inside the ground are two giant television screens, mounted on poles, that are rotated on non-match days to the plaza surrounding the stadium, and act as electronic advertising billboards. To further aid the costs of the new ground, all the stands have been sponsored—Coca-Cola, Continental, Vodafone and Nike sponsor the north, south, east and west structures respectively.

The Estadio do Dragao was an integral part of Euro 2004; it hosted the opening ceremony watched by millions, and held five matches all together in the summer tournament, including its opening match between hosts Portugal and eventual winners Greece, and the Greece–Czech Republic semi-final.

RIGHT: The Euro 2004 opening ceremony took place at the Dragao stadium in Porto before the match between host nation Portugal and Greece.

PAGE 218: A fine overhead view of the Dragao.

PAGE 219: Giant television screens and a transparent roof are just two distinguishing features of the Estadio Dragao.

100 YEARS
HYUNDAI
McDonald's
PORTO
MasterCard
T··Mobile·
JVC
HYUNDAI
Canon
UEFA

vodafone
vodafone

The Estadio Dragao in Porto was built to house up to 52,000 football fans during Euro 2004 at a cost of some 98 million euros. It is one of the finest stadiums in Europe.

PSV Eindhoven

Stadium:	Philips Stadion
Address:	Frederiklaan 10a, 5616 NH Eindhoven
Website:	www.psv.nl
Ground capacity:	36,500
Opening date:	1913
Most important games:	Euro 2000 Venue
Memorable moments:	PSV 3 AC Milan 1. Champions League semi-final, second leg. 4 May 2005

The industrial town of Eindhoven in the Netherlands is inextricably linked with electronic giants Philips—so much so that one of every five people in the city works for them. It was Philips that founded the local football team—Philips Sport Vereniging Eindhoven, or PSV Eindhoven for short—in August 1913. PSV were a company-sponsored team, giving the workers a hobby on the weekends, their formation also celebrating the Netherlands' 100 years of independence from France. They played on the site of the Philips Stadium from the club's inception, but the 36,000-capacity ground that exists today took time to create. It is now not only a football stadium but a 365 day a year venue housing offices, conference rooms, reception rooms and even bars and restaurants. This multi-purpose use is said to be a glimpse of the future.

The backing of Philips makes PSV the richest club in the Netherlands and as a result they and their fans enjoy significant perks, the best example being the gas heaters installed in the roof the stands ensuring the fans are warm even in the most arctic conditions. The stadium only had a 300-person limit as late as 1941 when it became 18,000. However, after being severely damaged months after in the second World War, repairs were made and the stadium's capacity was 22,000 in the early 1960s. One of the stadium's talking points in the 1980s was the distinctive 'Deckchair Stand', where it appeared the seats were set inside a cradle. Built in 1977, it only lasted a decade as cracks and faults were found literally months before the ten-year guarantee period set by the contractors was set to run out; it was subsequently replaced.

The Philips Stadion saw PSV win the UEFA Cup in 1978 when they triumphed 3–0 against French side Bastia in the second leg of the final. The stadium went on to host three matches at Euro 2000 and, although not considered huge by European standards, it has still been awarded four stars by UEFA, allowing it to host the UEFA Cup Final in 2006.

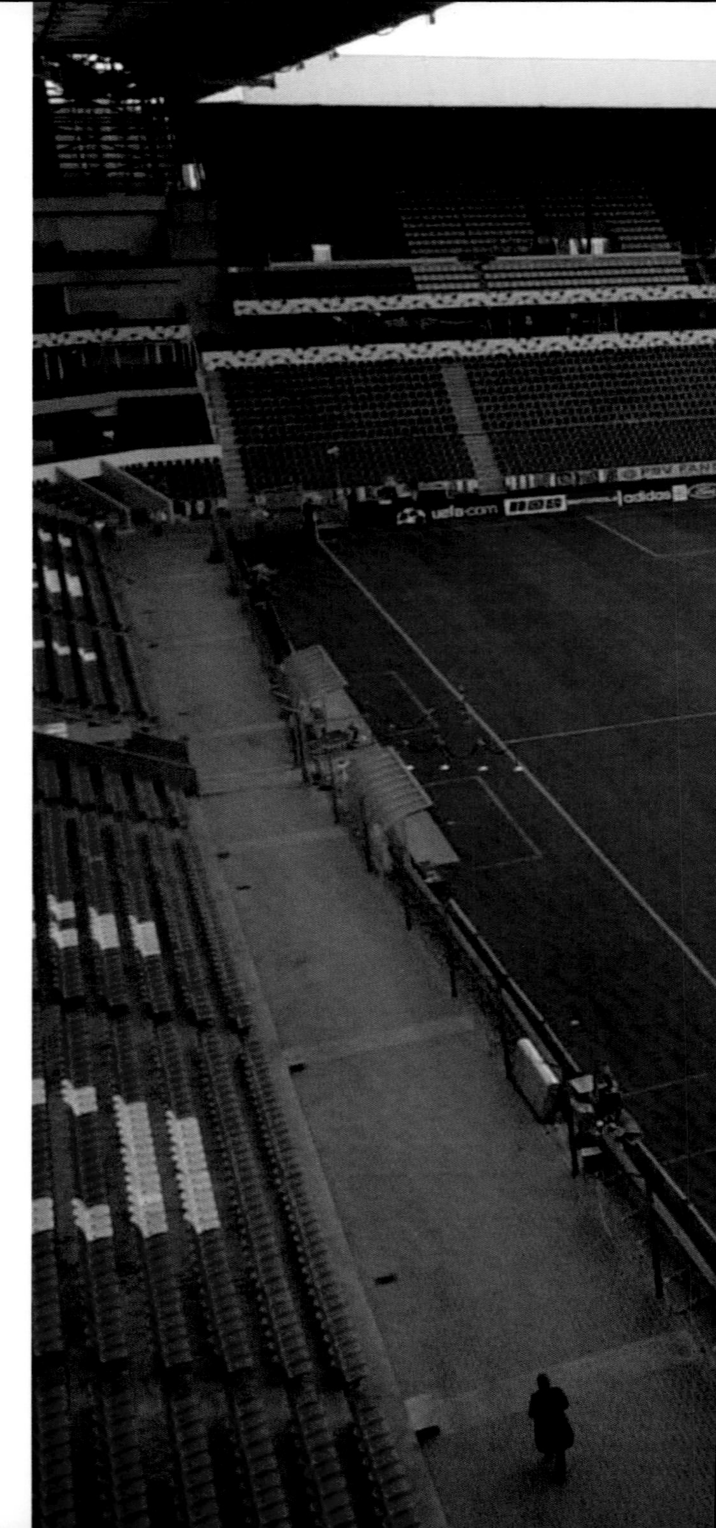

AMSTEL BEER
PlayStation.2
EUROCARD
FordFusion
MasterCard
FordFusion
AMSTEL BEER
PlayStation.2
EUROCAR

nutella
AMSTEL

LEFT: A packed Philips Stadion crowd enjoys the action of a Euro 2000 fixture.

ABOVE: Sweden and Turkey battle it out at Euro 2000 in front of 36,000 fans.

PREVIOUS PAGE: An empty but nevertheless impressive Philips Stadion, built with the electrical goods firm's money.

Rapid Wien (Vienna)

Stadium:	Gerhard Hanappi Stadion
Formerly:	Weststadion
Address:	Keisslergasse 6, 1140 Wien, Austria
Website:	www.skrapid.at
Ground capacity:	18,000
Opening date:	1977
Architect:	Gerhard Hanappi
Most important games:	Euro 2008 Venue
Memorable moments:	First Match: Rapid Vienna versus FK Austria. 10 May 1977

The Gerhard Hanappi Stadium in Austria has been home to Austrian Bundesliga club SK Rapid Vienna since 1977. Rapid, also known sometimes as 'Hutteldorf' after the location of their stadium in Vienna's 14th district, have regularly played in Europe and the Champions League in their stadium, while arch-rivals FK Austria have also been forced to play European ties there due to deficiencies in their own ground

Gerhard Hanappi, after whom the stadium is named, is a former Rapid player who held the record number of appearances for the Austrian national team. More interesting is the fact that Hanappi is also the stadium's architect, and it was named after him in the wake of his death from cancer, aged 51, in 1981. Through the design it is evident its creator had a footballing mind. The four stands are cantilever-roofed and afford a good view of the game, with two stands built behind the goals comparatively recently, and there is definitely no 'velodrome' or all-purpose track around the pitch.

At under 30 years old, the Gerhard Hanappi Stadium Rapid is relatively young stadium—too young, in fact, for Rapid to fit their 31 League title wins into their stay there. Every Rapid game features the 'Rapidviertelstunde', or rapid 15 minutes, where the Rapid fans will on their team to victory in the last quarter of an hour of a game. The ritual dates back to 1941, when Rapid overcame a three-goal deficit in the last 15 to win 4–3 against German club Schalke 04 in the German Cup Final.

The Gerhard Hanappi Stadion is one of the Austrian grounds to be used in the 2008 European Championships to be held in Austria and Switzerland, but no developments are planned at present.

RIGHT: 2004 view of the Gerhard Hanappi stadium during a EUFA cup first round game against Rubin Kazan.

PAGE 228: Vienna boasts one of FIFA's five-star grounds, the Ernst Happel Stadium. England players are seen training there in September 2004.

HYUNDAI
HYUNDAI
BURGENLAND
HYUNDAI
HYUNDAI
EDELSTEINE
carat-online.at
EDELSTEINE
carat-online.at
EDELSTEINE
EDELSTEINE
carat-online.at
EDELSTEINE
carat-online.at

BURGENLAND
HYUNDAI
HYUNDAI
BURGENLAND
HYUNDAI
HYUNDAI
AWD
AWD
AWD
AWD
BURGENLAND
BURGENLAND
LG
LG
LG
LG
LG

Real Madrid

Stadium:	El Estadio Santiago Bernabeu
Address:	Concha Espina 1, 28036 Madrid
Website:	www.realmadrid.com
Ground capacity:	80,000
Opening date:	14 December 1947, renovated 2003/04
Architect:	Luis Alemany Soler & Manuel Munoz Monasterio
Most important games:	World Cup 1982 Venue.
Memorable moments:	First Match: Real Madrid–OS Belenses

Considered by many the biggest team on the planet, Real Madrid have a stadium to match in the Santiago Bernabeu. Surprisingly, however, UEFA do not consider it part of Europe's elite and have not yet designated it a 5-star stadium.

Real moved into their current home, then known as the Estadio de Chamartin, in 1947, moving from their old ground of the same name. An initial capacity of 75,000 was increased by 45,000 just six years into Madrid's tenure, with the addition of a third tier of stands in 1953. In 1955, the ground was renamed after the club president that took Real to their current home and silverware started to accrue.

In 1957 Real Madrid won their second European Cup in front of their home fans, their first coming just a year before. They went on to take the sequence to five in a row. Brian Clough's Nottingham Forest won the second of their back-to-back European Cups at the Bernabeu in 1980.

Modernisation occurred in preparation for the 1982 World Cup, in which Madrid hosted four matches, bringing the capacity down to 90,000. The obvious highlight was the showpiece final in which Italy triumphed over West Germany. The Bernabeu surpassed the 100,000 mark once again in the early 1990s, but capacity was reduced to 74,000—full circle from when they originally moved in half a century earlier—when, in 1998, UEFA prohibited standing in their competitions.

Renovation in 2005 rounded up the spectator limit to an all-covered 80,000. There are plans to add a retractable roof, with Real Madrid still craving 5-star status for the home of galacticos Zidane, Beckham and Ronaldo.

RIGHT: An empty Santiago Bernabeu awaits the arrival of Valencia to challenge the Galacticos.

as
PEÑALBA
MADRID C.F.

MADRID

LEFT: The Estadio Bernabeu hosts a prestigious international friendly between Spain and England in November 2004.

ABOVE: Real's fans celebrate in central Madrid following the 2000 Champions League final in which they beat Valencia 3–0 to clinch an eighth European title.

Rosenborg

Stadium:	Lerkendal Stadion
Address:	Holtermannsv. 1, 7004 Trondheim
Website:	www.rbk.no
Ground capacity:	21,200
Opening date:	10 August 1947
Architect:	Selberg Arkitektkontor AS
Most important games:	Rosenborg 1 Arsenal 1. Champions League. 29 September 2004
Memorable moments:	Record attendance—28,569; Rosenborg versus Lillestrom, October 1985

The Lerkendal Stadium in Trondheim, Norway, was planned in 1933, but took 14 years to come into fruition due partly to the Second World War . When opened, it was home to local football club Rosenborg BK. Rosenborg didn't turn professional until a decade later, and in 1960 they 'did a Wimbledon' and won the Norwegian Cup. The club went up from there and won 13 consecutive Norwegian championships from 1992 till 2004.

The Lerkendal didn't reflect the ultra-successful team that played inside it, largely due to it having been constructed for a team that was nowhere near professional at the time. It began with temporary wooden stands, which were replaced with more permanent options in the 1960s, but the stadium then remained unchanged until 1996. The main north grandstand was then demolished and rebuilt, being renamed the Adidas Stand after its sponsors and the club's kit manufacturer

In 2000, after Rosenborg bought the stadium from the local council, the three remaining stands were rebuilt in the image of the Adidas Stand, creating four identical stands which aren't connected; these are characterised by their staggered roofing. The new stadium's construction was paid for by Rosenborg's many ventures into the Champions League, and their policy of selling their best players to foreign teams and replacing them with home-grown talent that still enables them to triumph domestically. Norway and Lyon striker John Carew is one example of this highly logical and profitable cycle. The new and improved Lerkendal was reopened in October 2002.

RIGHT: The natives of Trondheim enjoy a Champions League match against Boavista, October 1999.

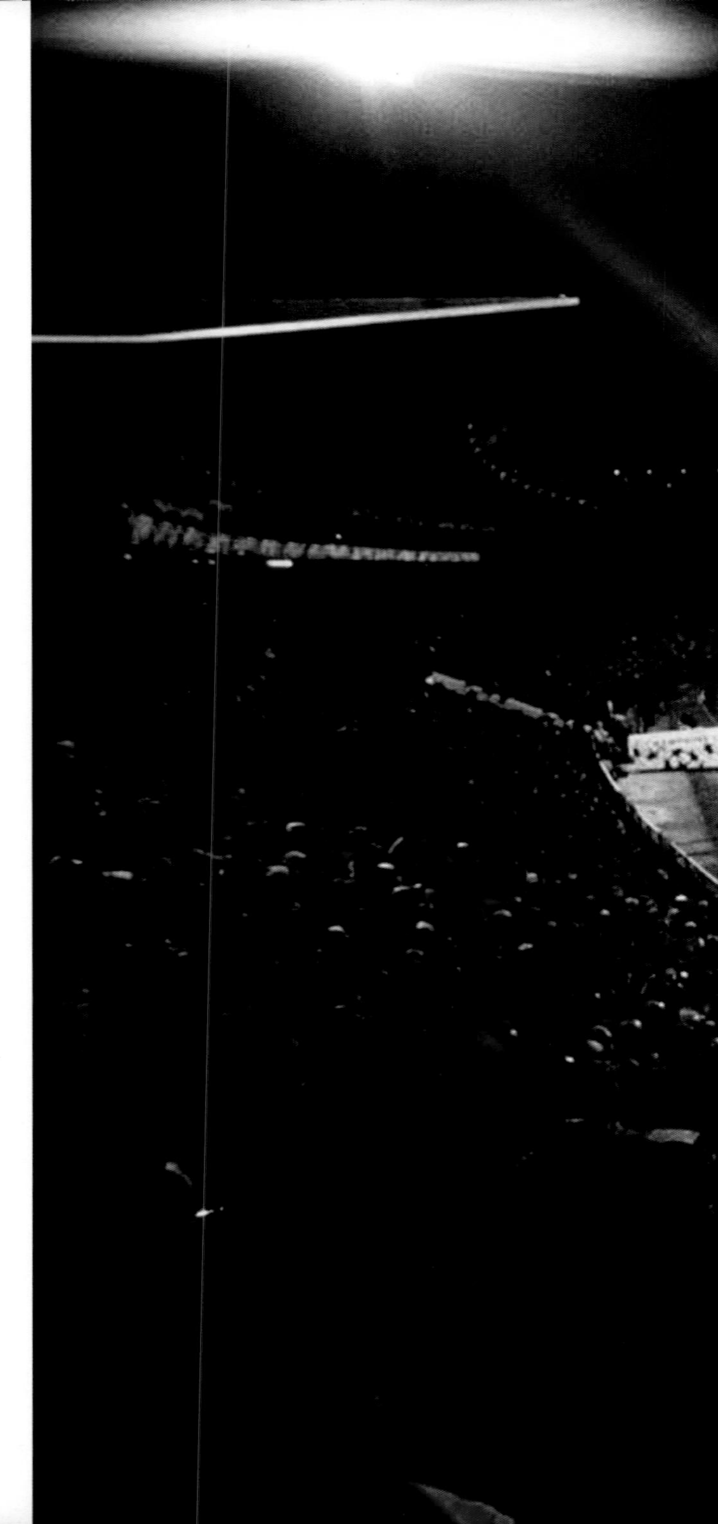

CHAMPIONS

Shakhtar Donetsk

Stadium:	New Shakhtar Stadion
Address:	Lenin Komsomol Park
Website:	www.shakhtar.com
Ground capacity:	50,000
Opening date:	February 2007
Architect:	Stephen Burrows and Jay Parrish
Most important games:	Not yet opened
Memorable moments:	Not yet opened

Following Shakhtar Donetsk's emergence as a regular competitor in both the UEFA Cup and the Champions League, and prising the Ukrainian Premier League title from rivals Dynamo Kiev, plans were put in place to reflect their new-found success. Not that the decision was taken lightly. No fewer than 20 drafts were viewed from architects with impressive CVs—many of whom had designed 5-star stadiums in the past.

The objective was to design a modern stadium that would fit into the picturesque landscape of the Lenin Komsomol park. The result was a 50,000 all-seater with the roof as its focal point. This slants from north to south, allowing more light through than usual thanks to the extensive use of glass. Work began in June 2005 and upon completion, tentatively scheduled for February 2007, it should be accredited with UEFA 5-star status, having fulfilled all the requirements

The New Shakhtar Stadion will include a shopping centre and a restaurant, allowing it to be used not just on matchdays but all week long. Shakhtar's current stadium, simply known as the Central Stadion Shakhtar, is used to innovation. It became only the second club within the Ukraine to employ floodlights in a match against CSKA Moscow in 1954. It has undergone several renovations in its history, the latest bringing capacity to 31,000 spectators, and is largely uncovered, apart from the main grandstand with its seats in Shakhtar's club colours of orange and black. It has witnessed some important matches in the Champions League with opponents such as Lazio, Arsenal, and Inter Milan.

RIGHT: The New Shakhtar Stadium will hold 50,000.

INSET: FC Shakhtar celebrate their victory against Odessa's Chornomorets, June 2005.

Sparta Prague

Stadium:	Toyota Arena
Formerly:	Letna Stadion; Stadion AC Sparta Praha
Address:	Milady Horakove 98, 170 82 Prague 7
Website:	www.sparta.cz
Ground capacity:	19,000
Opening date:	1933
Architect:	Kyril Mandel
Nickname:	Letna
Most important games:	Sparta Prague 1 Barcelona 0. European Cup 1992
Memorable moments:	April 1934. Fire ravages old incarnation of the stadium

Prague, the capital of the Czech Republic, is at the very centre of Europe. It is also home to the Toyota Arena, the stadium of Sparta Prague. Formerly known as the Letna Stadion (Summer Stadium) or Stadion AC Sparta Praha, it is also used by the Czech national football team for their big matches.

Although entry to matches is only approximately £3, the stadium is never usually full to 21,000 capacity, except for derby games between Sparta and fierce local rivals Slavia Prague. The fixture has a history of crowd trouble, and in 1934 the main grandstand was burnt to the ground, two days after a match against Slavia. It stayed that way for two years until Sparta constructed a concrete grandstand, which reopened in 1969 with a stadium capacity of 36,000. The stand's foundations are still in place today.

In 1994, club president Petr Mach ordered a redevelopment of the ground which transformed the Letna Stadion into the most modern all-seater sports venue in the Czech Republic. It now boasts two tiers of red and blue seats, though capacity is now a reduced 21,000. The arena was christened with another Sparta-Slavia derby. Away from match days, Sparta train at the Strahov Stadium, the largest stadium in the world, holding 250,000 people.

With further technical and structural developments in the pipeline for the future, funded by the naming deal struck with motor giants Toyota, and revenue from Sparta's regular outings in the UEFA Champions League, it appears the Toyota Arena will stay at the forefront of Czech stadia for some while to come.

RIGHT: UEFA told Sparta Prague to play their match against Arsenal behind partially closed doors in October 2005 after racism from Sparta fans.

Heineken ☆ Heineken

Sporting Lisbon

Stadium:	Estadio Jose Alvalade XXI
Address:	Rua Professor Fernando da Fonseca 1600-616, Lisbon
Website:	www.sporting.pt
Ground capacity:	52,000
Opening date:	July 2003
Architect:	Tomas Taveira
Nickname:	The bathroom
Most important games:	Staged quarter/semi-finals of Euro 2004
Memorable moments:	18 May 2005 UEFA Cup Final Sporting Lisbon 1 CSKA Moscow 3

Inspired by the Amsterdam Arena in Holland, this imposing oval stadium was conceived as one of the showcase venues for Euro 2004 and built at a cost of 79 million euros beside the ground of the same name it replaced. The colours of host club Sporting Lisbon are reflected in an exterior covered in light green tiles, leading to the unflattering nickname the 'bathroom'. Colours were carefully selected to give the stadium an identity, yellow signifying the structural elements, while the roof, suspended on tie-beams from four huge pillars—said to represent the giant masts of great Portuguese sailing ships—seems almost to float above the seating tiers. Beneath this canopy, black, blue, white, purple and orange seats create a harlequin-patterned effect.

Below the stands are seven levels that help make the stadium multi-functional for sport and music-related events. Indeed, it was designed with acoustics in mind —not to amplify the singing of fans but because of its use as a concert venue. Irish supergroup U2 appeared there in 2005 on their world tour. A large commercial area contains a multiplex cinema, shops, a health club and a bowling alley, maximising non-football income.

Situated less than 2km from the stadium of Sporting's rivals Benfica and ten minutes from the city centre, the Estadio Jose Alvalade was opened by a visit from Manchester United in August 2003: Sporting won 3–1. UEFA immediately showed its approval by awarding the stadium a five-star classification, ranking it among Europe's elite venues. One of the hardest-fought matches of Euro 2004 took place at the stadium on 20 June when the host country beat neighbours Spain. Portugal then sent fans into raptures ten days later, beating Holland 2–1 to reach the final. Their eventual conquerors Greece had graced the Jose Alvalade at the quarter-final stage, beating favourites France by a single goal.

The selection of the stadium to host the 2004–05 UEFA Cup Final inspired Sporting Lisbon. They only faltered at the last hurdle when CSKA Moscow beat them 3–1. Despite this disappointment, there will be many more major fixtures for Lisbon's football fans.

PREVIOUS PAGE, ABOVE AND RIGHT: Designed by architect Tomas Taveira, the Jose Alvade XXI has a capacity of 52,000 spectators and hosted five matches in Euro 2004.

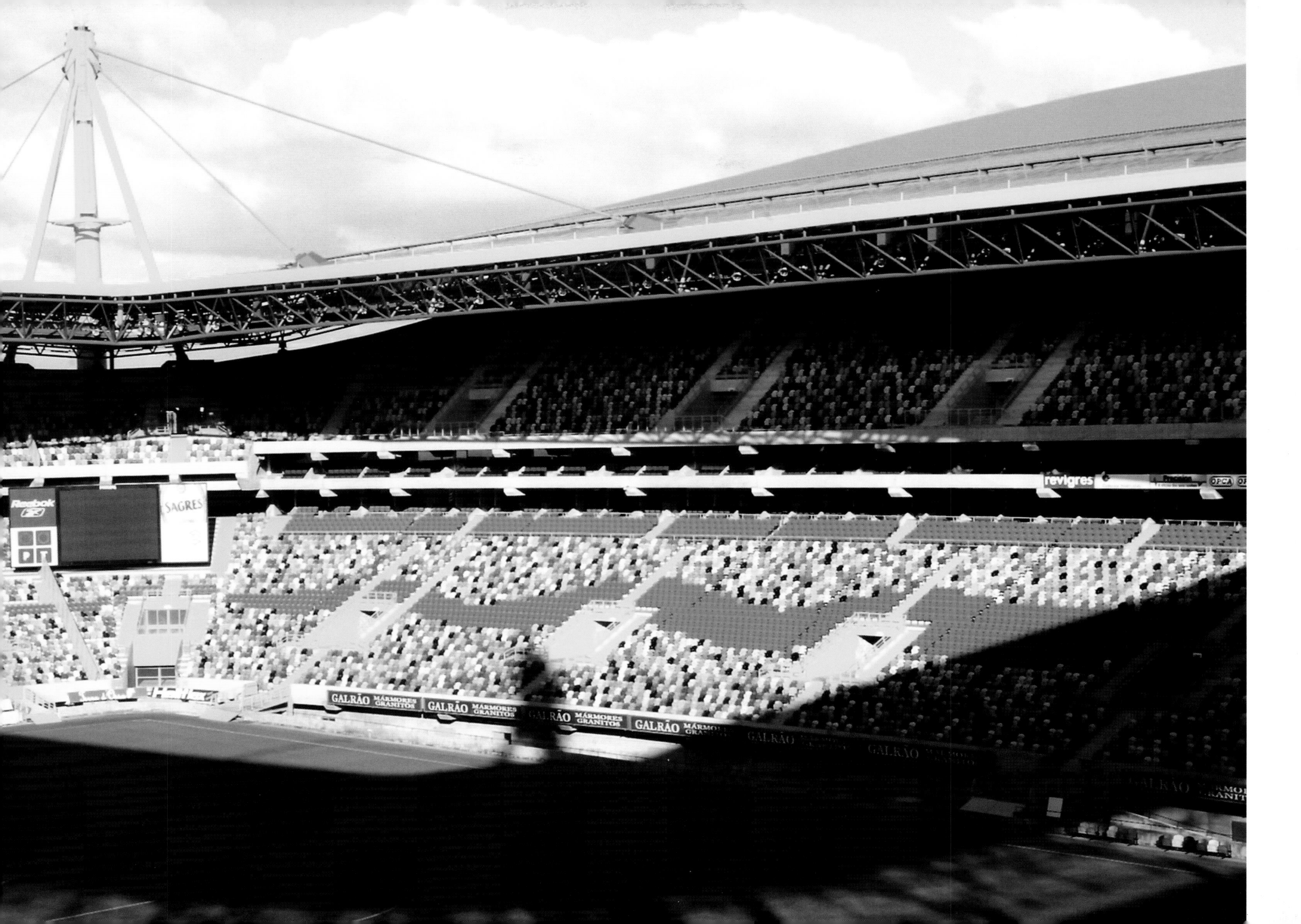
Reebok
SAGRES
GALRÃO MÁRMORES GRANITOS
GALRÃO MÁRMORES GRANITOS
GALRÃO MÁRMORES GRANITOS
revigres
OPCA

Standard Liege

Stadium:	Stade Maurice Dufrasne—Stade de Sclessin
Address:	Rue de la Centrale 2, 4000 Liege
Website:	www.standardliege.com
Ground capacity:	29,000
Opening date:	1910, renovated in 1998
Architect:	Adviesbureau R. Greisch S.A. and architectenbureau Audex
Nickname:	The Hell of Sclessin
Most important games:	Held three games in the European football Championships of 2000
Memorable moments:	Reopened in 1999 with a friendly international against Egypt

Home to Belgium's second largest team, Royal Standard de Liege, the Stade Maurice Dufrasne sits on the banks of the river Meuse in Sclessin, known as 'the burning city' because of its industrial nature. The stadium received its official title after Standard's former president of the same name.

Standard Liege have been at the Maurice Dufrasne for over 90 years, and the ground has hosted over 150 European matches against the likes of Real Madrid, Bayern Munich and Arsenal. Over the last 15 years, the Stade de Sclessin, as it is commonly known amongst fans, has undergone a transformation, with multi-tiered stands being erected and linked by a bright red cantilever roof which runs around three-quarters of the stadium, making it instantly recognisable. The ground was fine-tuned for Euro 2000 in which the Sclessin stadium held three group matches, including Germany versus Romania.

Further developments are planned for the future, including rebuilding the last stand and joining it to the other three, creating a fully covered stadium. Further work on the front facade is planned to include corporate facilities and a club shop. The most talked-about feature of the ground amongst the fans is how like an English stadium it is; there is no running track around the pitch as in most European stadia, so the fanatical fans of Liege are within touching distance of the players. This has earned the stadium the nickname of the 'Hell of Sclessin', and made it a venue opposing players are said to be nervous about visiting. The ground was officially reopened on 30 March 1999 with an international friendly between Belgium and Egypt.

RIGHT: The Stade de Sclessin in Liege, Belgium was one of the chosen venues for Euro 2000.

LE MUST
CIRIO
SECA
adidas

CIRIO
BUFFALO GRILL
BELGACOM
SECA
adidas

LEFT: Players do not enjoy visiting the 'Hell of Sclessin' when full to capacity with home support.

ABOVE: Viorel Moldovan (left) scores for Romania during the Euro 2000 match against Germany at Sclessin.

Steaua Bucharest

Stadium:	Ghencea Stadion
Address:	Bdul Ghencea 35, Sector 5 Bucuresti
Website:	www.Steauafc.com
Ground capacity:	28,000
Opening date:	April 1974, renovated 1996
Nickname:	The Romanian Football Temple
Most important games:	Steaua Bucharest 1 Liverpool 1. UEFA Cup Second round, first leg. 6 November 2003
Memorable moments:	First Match: FC Steaua 2 OFK Belgrade 2

The Ghencea Stadion in Ghencea, Bucharest, is home to Romanian outfit FC Steaua Bucharest, many-time Romanian champions who once went three years unbeaten in the league—a world record. The club started out as an army team, and were homeless for 27 years from their foundation until they moved into the Ghencea Stadion in 1974, and inaugurated the stadium with a 2–2 draw with Serbian outfit OFK Belgrade.

They are also the only Eastern European team to have won the European Cup, earning the impressive scalp of giants Barcelona when triumphing on penalties in Seville in 1986. Steaua proved they still had the giant-killing spirit as they dumped out holders Valencia in the 2004–05 UEFA Cup at the Ghencea. Although the stadium is used for many different sports, it focuses mainly on football due to Steaua's success in Europe; this is evident by the lack of a running track round the perimeter of the pitch. Only one stand in the stadium is covered, but it holds almost 30,000 people so atmosphere is not a problem.

Floodlights were added in 1991, while five years later the Ghencea underwent reconstruction and modernisation, filling the stadium with a sea of red and blue seats and giving it the reputation of being one of the 'fanciest stadiums' in Romania. However the pitch is not so fancy due to Romanian weather. In 2003 the managers of Southampton and Liverpool, the two English Premiership duo that visited the Ghencea in the UEFA Cup, blasted the pitch's condition. Liverpool's manager at the time, Gerard Houllier, even called it the worst pitch Liverpool had ever played on.

RIGHT AND FAR RIGHT: Supporters brave a heavy snowfall before the UEFA Cup match in Bucharest between Steaua and Villarreal at the Ghencea Stadium, March 2005.

STEAUA

Sturm Graz/Grazer AK

Stadium:	Graz-Liebenau Stadium
Formerly:	Arnold Schwarzenegger Stadium
Address:	Stadionplatz 1, 8041 Graz-Liebenau
Website:	www.sksturm.at
Ground capacity:	15,400
Opening date:	1997
Most important games:	Austria 2 Scotland 2. International Friendly. 17 August 2005
Memorable moments:	SK Sturm Graz 2 Glasgow Rangers 0. Champions League. 25 October 2000

Though the stadium, named after the internationally famous movie star born in the town it serves, has only been around since 1997, the clubs that share it have a longer if not more illustrious history. Sturm Graz formed in 1909, while Grazer AK were formed seven years earlier. Both clubs ply their trade in the Austrian Bundesliga.

The two clubs who now share a stadium enjoy a healthy rivalry, the evenness of which is testified to by the fact that in summer 2005 the playing record in derby games read: Grazer AK 44 Sturm 39, with 40 matches drawn. The goals tally was similarly close, 166 to 161.

It has to be an impressive ground to persuade fans to co-exist, and it is. Its all-seater capacity of 15,450 sees every fan provided with protection from the elements, while an opulent 40-metre lounge takes care of VIPs. In addition there are 60 seats for disabled persons and their escorts.

The pitch is served by no fewer than three underground springs, so is always well watered, even in a drought. In case of bad weather, there is undersoil heating to defrost the pitch; this can be set high enough to melt snow if necessary. Instead of a fence the pitch is surrounded by a ditch feet feet wide.

Six dressing rooms are luxuriously equipped with a spa pool, baths, showers and toilets. There is also an adjoining warm-up room, while a video system allows the teams to discuss last-minute tactics.

Spectators can gain access to 27 sectors of the ground via fully electronically controlled entrances, while there are 12 ticket windows. The stadium boasts a 640-space underground car park, but free park and ride operates on production of a match ticket.

Right: The stadium in Graz was named for Arnold Schwarzenegger as seen here. However, following the governor of California's approval of the execution of Stanley "Tookie" Williams, Austrian politicians campaigned to have his name removed. Schwarzenegger responded by removing the right to use his name. Until a sponsor is found, the stadium will be known as the Graz-Liebenau Stadium.

CHWARZENEGGER STADION GRAZ-LIEBENAU
TABAK
LOTTO TOTO LOTTO
UTOMAT

Valencia

Stadium:	Estadio Mestalla
Address:	Avda. de Suecia 46010 Valencia
Website:	www.valenciacf.es
Ground capacity:	55,000
Opening date:	20 May 1923
Most important games:	World Cup 1982 Venue
Memorable moments:	First Match: Valencia 1 Levante 0

Stadiums today are no stranger to name changes, with clubs desperate for the financial benefits selling the rights to big corporations. Other times, past or present legends at the club are celebrated. Having changed their ground's name and then reverted to the original, maybe Valencia should consider renaming the Estadio Mestalla the Phoenix, as it seems to continually rise from the ashes.

When first built in 1923, the stadium, named after a nearby river, had a modest capacity of 17,000, but this was quickly increased to 25,000. The Mestalla was severely affected by the Spanish Civil War, largely because of its proximity to the Valencian docks, and was repaired in 1940. Success on the field in the 1940s helped Valencia gradually improve the ground. It was renovated in the 1950s and when the strikingly roofed main stand was built in 1954 capacity rose to 45,000. Once again, however, disaster struck. The flood of 1957 damaged the Mestalla, but the ground returned to normality two years later, now complete with floodlights. 1962 and '63 saw consecutive Inter Cities Fairs Cup final victories in front of home fans when Valencia crushed compatriots Barcelona 6–2, and saw off Dinamo Zagreb 2–0 the following year. Both ties were two-leg affairs.

The end of that decade saw the stadium renamed in honour of former president Luis Casanova Giner, who helped bring Valencia's success following the Civil War. In 1978 the pitch was lowered significantly in order to increase the ground's capacity, with an eye on the forthcoming World Cup. The Luis Casanova Stadium went on to host all three of Spain's first group stage matches, the national team enjoying mixed fortunes with a win, a draw and a defeat. In 1994 the stadium reverted to its original name of Mestalla, and there are still calls from the Spanish public for it to become the official home of the national team.

RIGHT: John Carew of Valencia beats David Seaman of Arsenal to score the winning goal in their Champions League quarter-final at the Mestalla Stadium, Valencia, in 2001.

PAGE 252: Valencia's new coach Claudio Ranieri answers journalists' questions during his official presentation in Mestalla Stadium in Valencia, 8 June 2004.

adidas

bigfoot
VALENCIA
MARCA
UGARTE

Wisla Krakow

Stadium:	Stadion Wisla
Address:	22, Reymonta St., Krakow
Website:	www.wisla.krakow.com.pl
Ground capacity:	10,440
Opening date:	1922
Most important games:	Wisla Krakow 3 Panathinaikos 1 European Champions League qualifier 9 August 2005
Memorable moments:	Glasgow Celtic in the UEFA Cup

Wisla Krakow have been Polish champions 11 times at the time of writing. They were founded in 1907 by a Dr Tadeusz Konczynski who, the previous year, organised a football tournament in the city of Krakow. Wisla is thus is one of the oldest football clubs in Poland and is known as 'The White Star'. The furthest they have ventured in European competition was in 1977–78 when they reached the European Cup (now Champions League) quarter-finals.

The current ground was opened in 1953 and the record attendance of 45,000 came when they hosted Glasgow Celtic in the UEFA Cup. At the present ground, spectators can gather behind only one of the goals, at the Reymonta St end, the other being closed. The majority are seated in the 4,000-capacity Jordan's Park stand. The grass playing surface was replaced in summer 2003, and there is under-soil heating, crucial to play football in the inhospitable Polish weather, but spectators in all but the VIP stand are expected to brave the elements, there being no cover. The current floodlights were installed in summer 2002.

The stadium is being rebuilt (as the Stadion Wisly) to host 30,000 people in four roofed stands. It will satisfy UEFA regulations, and will be able to host Champions League matches. The reconstruction process began in November 2004.

The idea of erecting a new Polish National Stadium in Krakow to house some 28,000 spectators was mooted in 1998, but was abandoned soon after. Impressive models do, however, exist.

Cable producers Telefonika, acquired the club in 1998. Wisla's most famous recent player is Maciej Zurawski, who signed for Celtic in 2005.

RIGHT: Targino Tiago scores for Vitoria Guimaraes against Wisla in their UEFA Cup match in Krakow, September 2005.

PAGE 254: The new Wembley stadium under construction in May 2005. It was due to host its first match, the FA Cup final, in May 2006.

expekt
zakłady/kasyno/poker

Index